THE
RELATION OF SCULPTURE
TO
ARCHITECTURE

THE
RELATION OF SCULPTURE
TO
ARCHITECTURE

BY

T. P. BENNETT, A.R.I.B.A.

Cambridge :
at the University Press
1916

CAMBRIDGE
UNIVERSITY PRESS

University Printing House, Cambridge CB2 8BS, United Kingdom

Cambridge University Press is part of the University of Cambridge.

It furthers the University's mission by disseminating knowledge in the pursuit of
education, learning and research at the highest international levels of excellence.

www.cambridge.org
Information on this title: www.cambridge.org/9781107593824

© Cambridge University Press 1916

First published 1916
First paperback edition 2015

A catalogue record for this publication is available from the British Library

ISBN 978-1-107-59382-4 Paperback

PREFACE

I HAVE fully described the purpose of this book in the Introduction, and the description which will there be found needs no amplification in the Preface. I must, however, acknowledge the assistance I have received from many friends and generous strangers since the beginning of 1913, when I first decided upon the scope of the work.

Outstanding names which call for particular mention are the following:—Sir Aston Webb, Sir Thomas Brock, Sir William Goscombe John, Mr Hamo Thorneycroft, Mr E. Guy Dawber, Messrs Méwes & Davis, Messrs Vincent Harris & Moody, Mr Arthur Monger, Mr H. W. Bennett, M. René Claes, The Athenaeum Club, H.M. Office of Works, the Proprietors of *The American Architect*, The Swetland Publishing Company, The Pan-American Union, Mr Alexander Stiles, whose modelling will be seen in Fig. 72, Mr John Angel, who designed the Sculpture Group in Fig. 27, and Miss Isabel Strother, who devoted many hours of very valuable time to the critical examination of my manuscript before it was submitted to the Press.

And finally my thanks are due to my publishers, who have been of the greatest assistance in obtaining illustrations, arranging type and setting and doing their utmost in every way to meet my views with regard to the details of production.

T. P. BENNETT.

14, GREAT JAMES STREET,
BEDFORD ROW, W.C.
October 1915.

CONTENTS

CHAPTER I

INTRODUCTION

CHAPTER II

THE TREATMENT AND PLACING OF SCULPTURE IN
THE HISTORIC PERIODS

CONTENTS vii

CHAPTER III

DECORATIVE SCULPTURE

(1) *Intimately related to Architecture*

CHAPTER IV

DECORATIVE SCULPTURE

(2) *Applied to Architectural Forms*

CHAPTER V

THE PLACING AND SURROUNDINGS OF MONUMENTS

CONTENTS

CHAPTER VI

THE SMALL MONUMENT

Limitations of Size and Cost—The Selection of the Material—The Intro-
duction and Use of Lettering—Colour—Originality of Conception as Opposed
to Originality of Detail—Variety in Treatment—Symbolic Ornament—Treat-
ments involving the Use of the Bust—Single Standing Figure Monuments—
The Design of a Pedestal to suit the Figure—The Base of the Pedestal—Single
Seated Figure Monuments—Unity in the Complete Design—Two Figure
Monuments—Small Three Figure Groups—Bas-relief Compositions in small
Monuments—Suitability of Rustic and Sylvan Surroundings—Rococo Ele-

CHAPTER VII

LARGER MONUMENTS

Equestrian Monuments—The Treatment of the Horse—The Pedestal—
The Base of the Pedestal—The Enrichment of the Pedestal—Freedom in
Design—Large Figure Compositions—Square and Circular Pedestals—The
Introduction of a Form Based on the Obelisk—The Obelisk as the Basis of
Design—Columnar Monuments—Consideration given to General Design—
The Shaft—The Capital—The Base—The Triumphal Arch—The Colossal

CHAPTER VIII

LARGE MONUMENTAL LAY-OUTS

Importance of the General Scheme—National Symbolism Introduced into
the Conception—Domination of the Architecture—The Setting—The Kaiser
Monument at the German Corner—The Kaiser Monument, Porta, Westphalia—
The Kaiser Monument on the Kyffhauser—The Kaiser Monument, Berlin—
The Victor Emmanuel Monument, Rome—The Robert Fulton Memorial, New
York—The Soldiers' and Sailors' Monument, New York—The Albert Memorial,
London—The Queen Victoria Memorial, London—English Monumental Design

CHAPTER IX

CONCLUSION

Intercourse between Sculptors and Architects—The Appointment of an
Artist and the Apportionment of Responsibility—The Claims of the Sculptor

LIST OF ILLUSTRATIONS

CHAPTER I

INTRODUCTION

ONE of the most certain signs of vitality in the architecture of
England to-day is the growing use of sculpture upon
important buildings in various parts of the country.
In all the greatest periods of their history, architecture and sculpture have gone hand in hand, and the exponents of the one have had a very intimate knowledge of the principles and have been in sympathy with the ideals of the other. Frequently the connection has been much closer than this, and the necessary training and ability have been found in the same artist, first to design the building and afterwards to take mallet and chisel and carve the more important figures with which the structure is adorned.

The growing use of Sculpture.

The position of Phidias with respect to the buildings he embellished was, as is well known, not like that of the modern sculptor who, with very little architectural knowledge, models a figure to certain dimensions given him, but must have been that of a man whose wide experience upon buildings enabled him to hold a position at least equal to that of the architect. The internal evidence provided in the perfect relation established between sculpture and architecture would have been sufficient to proclaim the fact, were it not otherwise known. His was the mind which decided the relief necessary, the type of modelling required, and the best disposition of the masses to obtain the harmonious effect which the final composition presents.

Phidias and Greek architecture.

This intimate relation between the two arts is continued in Gothic times, when the mason seems to have been the authority to whom all turned for the solution of problems of construction or of design. The mere fact that he is described as a master-mason or by some other title is

Sculpture in the Gothic Period.

neither here nor there. To a large extent he filled the office both of the sculptor and the architect.

In the Renaissance Period in Italy, the same state of things obtained. The giants of art who flourished in the glorious days of the fifteenth and sixteenth centuries were brilliant exponents of both sculpture and architecture; even more—they were often past masters of painting as well. So much is this the case, that had the work of Michael Angelo, the most famous of them all, been the work of three separate men—a painter, a sculptor and an architect—each would have been acclaimed a genius in his own particular sphere. It is only a logical outcome of the guiding influence of one master-mind over the planning, design and ornamentation of the building that each harmonises with the other in a marked degree, and that the sculpture is not only good as sculpture, but good as decoration also.

Sculpture in the Renaissance in Italy.

In this connection it should be borne in mind that it is quite possible to have beautiful modelling which may be utterly bad decoration. It is necessary that the sculpture should not only be satisfactory in itself, but should be in sympathy with its surroundings and partake of a similar character.

Subservience to architectural forms.

Although the Parthenon may be one of those masterpieces of the world which can satisfy the critic from any point of attack, yet it will be admitted that the groups of sculpture with which it is adorned are infinitely better as decorative works (for which they were intended) than they can ever appear as studio or museum groups. The peculiar flat surfaces and the square modelling of the detail, both of the drapery and of the figure, are strongly reminiscent of the surrounding architectural forms. If the paradox may be allowed, the sculpture is more architectural than it is sculpturesque.

It is at first sight somewhat extraordinary that a reference to the totally different groups in Gothic work finds this harmony between the forms of the sculpture and the architecture equally marked. How striking is the similarity between the stiff vertical folds of the drapery on the Gothic figure and the lines of the shafts and mouldings upon pier and pinnacle and vault! They seem to re-echo each other more strongly or more faintly as the architecture or the figure is the more important. It may be taken as an absolute necessity of decorative sculpture that this harmony of form should exist. The sculptor of to-day is often called upon to provide ornament of various kinds, including the use of the figure, when the design of the building is already complete; even, it may be, after building operations have begun and stones have been placed in position with the boasting already upon them, so that the limits of the enrichment are defined within unalterable boundaries, thus cramping the actual detail of the ornament as well as the imagination of the artist.

It seems a necessity of modern conditions that the work of the sculptor and the architect should be embodied in two different personalities, and since this is so, when the sculptor is designing a group to enrich a building he must for the time being render his ideas and translate his personality into the key adopted by the architect.

When monumental work is in question, because of the more ideal nature of the group and the relative increase in the importance of the sculpture, this subservience to architectural forms is not so necessary; in fact, it is incumbent upon the architect to make his design for pedestal or setting recognise the proximity and requirements of the sculpture, and the detail which he employs will be modified to a great extent. The architecture has no longer to serve commercial needs and the demands of practical construction, but is employed as a foil to plastic forms and as a means of connection between them and the surrounding objects, whether those objects are buildings or the lawns and flowers of the garden.

Subservience to sculpture forms.

The exact nature of these surroundings will have a considerable influence upon the design of the pedestal or other architectural portion of the monument. A scheme which would be perfectly suitable in the freedom of a park might be most incongruous in the confines of a city " place " or when subjected to the severe limitations of a street junction.

The influence of surroundings.

Sculpture of itself will always possess a great attraction for artistic people. The phrase "the human form divine" which sometimes slips so glibly from the tongue contains a reference to the greatest of all beauties of nature—a beauty which never palls, however insistent it may become; which is never commonplace, even with the greatest of proverbial familiarity. Whether, as a separate entity, the group of sculpture is placed upon a specially-prepared pedestal in the

The attraction of sculpture.

building ; whether it forms an integral portion of the structure ; or whether it has importance of its own—as in monumental work—it always constitutes a virile centre of interest. It follows, therefore, if it will attract so much attention that a great and beautiful thought should be embodied in the group, and that its forms should bear the closest examination consistent with the purpose in view. If it is in a building, it is necessary that strong expression should be given to the relation of the masses to each other and to their position, and it should form the subject of some quality, incident or fact specially connected with the structure.

Lettering should always be attached giving the subject which

The statement of the subject. the figure represents. It is a great mistake to leave any doubt in the mind of the spectator as to whether the sculptor wishes to convey by his group, for example, "Invention," "Engineering," or "Manufacture." Each could very reasonably be represented by means of a figure holding a model of a piece of machinery, and a similar group would be equally appropriate to all. But if it is distinctly called either one or the other, at once a clue is given to the purpose for which the building exists. In the first instance it would suggest a great technical university, in the second a society numbering among its members many of the most distinguished men of a great profession, and in the third a hive of industry throbbing with the beat of many pistons, the whirring of wheels, and the steady drone of belting. In the same way, when the group is part of a monumental work it should not content itself merely with giving the features of the man, but should in addition tell part of the grand story of his life work.

The inflated importance placed in recent years upon originality

The modern cry for originality. of any kind has led to the production of a number of sculptured figures and groups which can only be described as the result of freakish ideas striving, at any cost, to obtain new forms. It is one of the worst phases through which any art can be called upon to pass. In the case of Music and Painting, its influence is bad enough, but in these Arts no structural laws are broken. In the course of time the paintings are destroyed or relegated to secluded positions known only to the few, and by those few rightly ignored. The music may have a fashionable season or two, but it very soon ceases to be played, and, like the painting, becomes merely a matter of historic fact—

simply a phase which must be studied by that small section of the public who are making music their profession in life.

But sculpture, like architecture, is a concrete art and has structural form, and also, of necessity, a permanence which neither music nor painting possesses. It is generally placed in a specially-prepared, conspicuous position, and in the ordinary course of affairs remains undisturbed for a considerable period. Every effort is made to protect it from possible depredations by man and from the destructive effect of the elements. It is doubly necessary, therefore, that innovations introduced by any individual exponent should have very careful consideration before they receive anything like general adoption. The precision of square outline, of well-defined mass is invaluable, but when the limbs and torso come to be composed of cubical shapes cut sharply into one another surmounted by a rectangular head, the utmost license will not allow that such were these shapes as seen by the sculptor and that the carving is a natural expression of his personality. In some of the modern German sculpture the heads of figures are bent around so that they are at right angles to the body, with the face looking directly downwards—sometimes bent to an even greater angle than this, inclined inwards—an attitude rendered possible by the introduction of a neck about twice as long as the normal. Wild compositions showing figures curling around under great masses of masonry or under oriel windows three stories in height, are equally to be deprecated, as are also figures placed on various portions of buildings without any visible means of support. Such figures are sometimes, apparently suspended in mid-air and attached to the structure by means of drapery or some inevident and mysterious force behind.

All this outrage upon pure form and scholarly treatment for the sake of so-called originality is a false attitude to adopt, either from an artistic or from a practical point of view. If an artist has personality he need never fear that it will remain unexpressed. If the work is natural to himself and carefully studied it cannot help appealing to others. The greater his personality and the more natural his expression, the greater will be this effect, although it may happen, as is only to be expected, that to the man himself the work seems a simple and natural treatment—the inevitable and only possible way of rendering the subject or solving the problem presented.

It is a well-known fact in many things far removed from

Simple ex-pression of personality.

architecture and sculpture that beautiful simplicity is frequently much more costly than the greatest ostentation. So it is that a perfect and original work which yet bears the unmistakable mark of natural expression is infinitely rarer than a rich design obviously produced by an effort. The reason is not far to seek. In the former case, the artist has studied cause and effect so long, so carefully, and with such good result that the right thing to do springs intuitively to his mind. Work such as this which has become accomplished and yet has retained its purity and natural expression is extremely rare and is not produced by the ordinary practitioner in artistic crafts.

Unfortunately the ordinary student goes through his training noting a good point here and a bad one there, until, having unconsciously separated a certain amount of wheat from the chaff, reserved a little good from the one and taken warning from the other, he ultimately reaches some passable level of skill himself. But it is only a mediocre level after all. It is not so high as it ought to be, and until all artists study upon logical lines with definite aim they cannot hope to see English sculpture and English architecture foremost among that of the countries of the world.

It must of course be conceded that one man cannot give know-
The purpose ledge to another, possibly even he cannot do more
in view. than make a few general assertions, yet the careful examination of all available examples must reveal certain more or less definite facts which will act as a basis for individual study and save a large amount of that fruitless search for useful information which has such deadly effect upon the energy and nerves of many a life-long student.

With this end in view the author has collected examples of the various features under discussion, classified them, and from their examination made deductions of certain facts which seem to be established.

As far as possible, mere personal assertion has been avoided as serving no useful end, and practically every statement made can be upheld by an existing example. For all this, it is not contended for an instant that the treatments here suggested are the only ones possible—in fact, during the course of detailed investigation into the subject even more convincing proof has been found, if such were needed, that an apparently hopeless feature can be turned into a design of the greatest brilliance if the correct way of handling it can be found.

But although an endeavour has been made to avoid dogmatic assertion, it is inevitable that personal individuality should have governed the choice of examples and directed the conclusions which are drawn from their study. It is hoped that readers will take the expression of these views as a sincere attempt to improve the standard and purity of sculpture on buildings and the design of monuments, and condone any offence to their personal feelings. Reference has been made to many examples of work executed in other countries, not because they are necessarily better than those in our own, but because they contain new thoughts, suggestions and ideas, which, grafted on to those already in existence, may help to widen the outlook of the artist and give him a greater range of treatment than he before possessed. Lack of imagination seems to have been rather a fault during the last decade and it is very necessary that it should be remedied without delay.

Both France and Germany have recently produced some extremely interesting work showing very versatile treatment in composition and detail, and the study of the examples from these countries and from Belgium will reveal a large amount of very interesting material.

Modern work in France and Germany.

The scholarship of the modern American is another notable feature, and shows how a systematic study of ancient examples at least prevents the production of really bad work. It leads to restraint and consideration in the use of ornament, and tends to cause the arts of sculpture and architecture to progress upon particularly sane and useful lines. Most of the best work now being produced in the United States shows evidence of most careful thought and accurate proportion. The placing of decorative sculpture is frequently excellent and the detail almost above reproach. The situation of monuments is receiving careful attention and the haphazard positions which have ruined the possibility of proper appreciation in many notable instances should be eliminated in the future.

In the United States.

The various chapters have been carefully divided into groups and sub-headings to facilitate reference, and overlapping has been avoided as far as possible. Some small amount was in places inevitable, but it is hoped that where this occurs the marginal reference will make its position clear and prevent confusion.

The division of the chapters.

CHAPTER II

THE TREATMENT AND PLACING OF SCULPTURE IN THE HISTORIC PERIODS

THE extraordinary accuracy of the reflection of national characteristics shown in the various historic styles of architecture must always have a great fascination for the artist whose studies take him beyond the bare facts of history.

This accuracy is found no less in the ornament, the sculpture or the monument than it is in the disposition of the parts of a building or the treatment of its façade. It is, in fact, possible that the individual piece of ornament or group of sculpture, being smaller, is more fully under the control of its creator and may reflect local variations and individual temperaments to an extent impossible with the great mass of the architecture.

The general forms and positions adopted for particular features were dictated by the aims of the artist for the time being. Thus, in Egyptian art are found either a vast series of figures employed in such a manner as to instruct the people and portray to them the great truths taught by religion, or colossal sculptured figures of kings, which serve to show the glory and veneration accorded to the deified monarch after his decease.

In Greece it may be said that neither of these considerations had any place. Greek sculpture emanated from a pure desire to produce perfected types of human physical beauty, and the whole trend of Greek design is towards that end. The portrayal of myths is sometimes indulged in, it is true, but it is more a portrayal of fancy and has not the definite and serious instructive purpose of Egyptian work.

Some of these points will be touched upon in each division to show how the thoughts, aims and purpose of each Period dictated the forms which the sculpture should adopt. The degree of perfection attained depended upon the development of the people artistically and socially; the extent of learning; the appreciation and support which the arts received; besides being affected by wars and disturbances which often had no connection, in the first place, with the peoples whose art they were eventually to influence.

There is one great and essential difference between the development of most of the styles previous to the Renaissance and those which developed from it. In the early civilizations, owing to internal seclusion and lack of travel, there was, broadly speaking, only one possible pathway open to the artist, and that was to build or to carve in the traditional style. After the Renaissance this limitation of style began to disappear and successful design became much more a matter of individual genius.

The architecture and the sculpture of the historic styles, and also those of foreign countries, are at the present day available to the student in a far more complete manner than has ever been the case before. The age of blind tradition has gone, but while the influence of tradition cannot ever be absent, conscious selection and definite learning have become rivals with it in importance, and if the work of contemporary sculptors and architects is to rival the masterpieces of antiquity, it can only be accomplished by the exercise of these qualities of judgment and scholarship.

An historic survey, however, reveals other and equally valuable material. In the styles of antiquity are found prototypes of many features employed in modern work, and these prototypes are often of far more value to the imaginative man than are the completed products of contemporary minds. In the prototype he can see the germ of an idea quite undeveloped, quite foreign to the requirements of the moment, but in such a condition that his mind may seize upon it and weave around it an entirely new conception.

Each country, also, has developed monumental forms which have in many cases remained untouched by later civilizations and so, by turning to each style or period, suggestions and new forms are revealed which may have possibilities for future use.

Egyptian Period, B.C. 4777—30.

The earliest civilization whose work has directly affected modern art is that of Egypt, and many qualities found in Egyptian work have a counterpart in modern life. The simplicity, directness and conservative qualities which are stamped indelibly upon everything the Egyptian did are also characteristics of the English people, and it follows that at times the work wants but little transposition before it is ready for use. Many of the forms used show a strength of treatment coupled with fine restraint which gives them an almost majestic character.

The low relief ornament and figures of the temple front and elsewhere suggest that richness and texture might be gained in certain places by low bas-relief carving introduced without disturbing the breadth of the architecture. At the other extreme are the colossal figures which sometimes adorned the spaces between the doorways. Such a group of openings as that presented by the theatre-front might form the field for decoration upon similar lines.

The composition of the winged globe and the vulture with outstretched wings frequently employed over an opening is of itself an excellent piece of detail, the high relief in the centre making a brilliant focal point which is surrounded by the low richness of the other carving. Many birds and animals besides the vulture received most decorative treatment, and special mention may be made of the sphinx and the hawk.

Lettering formed an important part in the decorative scheme, but while inscriptions of enormous length would never now be used, yet necessary directions, names and titles, might often be made part of the ornamentation of the structure to its great advantage.

The custom of placing obelisks in front of the pylons of the temple is worthy of attention. The great mass of masonry in the pylon, which might otherwise have passed unnoticed, is forced into prominence by the juxtaposition of the thin and delicate outline of the obelisk, while this in itself receives the utmost value by contrast with the unbroken wall-surface behind.

In addition to its decorative value, the obelisk is a most
Monuments. valuable monumental form. It will always have a distinction of its own and should be employed in monumental schemes far more often than it is at present. Reference to some successful modern examples is made in Chapter VI.

The pyramid, which, as used in Egypt, upon a large scale, is one of the most wasteful monumental structures ever invented by man, might yet, in small schemes, be a valuable feature, and its claims are at any rate worth consideration.

Babylonian Period, B.C. 4000—1290.
Assyrian Period, B.C. 1290—538.
Persian Period, B.C. 538—332.

These three periods, although divided by the historians in recognition of the political changes in the country, in reality represent three phases of the architecture of one people, and bear great similarity to one another in technique, design and composition.

Assyrian work (under which name, for the sake of convenience,

Fig. 1.   Portion of a Bas-relief from the Palace of Assur-bani pal, now in the British Museum.

it may be described) will in parts repay careful study.   Its greatest glory was undoubtedly the bas-relief (Fig. 1).   Many of the compositions are indeed excellent, while the detail and craftsmanship display a study of nature and a mastery of representation which the greatest of modern men may well envy. Lions, with great manes or of the so-called "lioness" type, were perhaps carried to the greatest perfection.   The representation of men is archaic and stiff and of little use to modern work.

Some of the sculptured ornament of which there are remains is interesting, but much of it was carried to a greater degree of perfection at a later period by the Greeks.

Of monumental forms there are few. The Assyrian type of
obelisk with a flat top and panels on the sides carved
with bas-relief—a variation upon the more familiar
Egyptian—is in some ways more suited to the shapes adopted in
modern design. It may be used with effect upon a scale which would
be quite impossible with the previous type. Size is of itself a
necessary accompaniment to the effective use of the Egyptian form.

Monuments.

The great mound or plateau upon which the palaces were
built has found an echo in a similar feature employed in modern
German monumental work (see Fig. 102), but although originally
used purely as an adjunct, it may now be considered as a feature
of importance in design. Its original purpose of bringing the
palace into prominence by raising it well above the level of the
surrounding plain, suggests its function in a modern scheme.

Greek Period, B.C. 500—146.

Sculpture in the Greek Period was applied to buildings with
the greatest care and discrimination, and for that reason should
receive the highest and most extensive attention.

Unlike the custom which afterwards prevailed in the Gothic
Period of creating richness by the use of a profusion of figures,
the Greeks used few and disposed those few in carefully-selected
positions. Thus the whole building was crowned by a great band
of ornament composed of alternating triglyph and metope; the
relief of the carving upon the metope was so adjusted that it
maintained the degree of strength suggested by the projection
of the triglyph. At each end of the temples appeared great
groups of figures in the pediments, carved in the round so as
not to be in danger of losing their proper value from the strong
contrasts of light and shade produced by the colonnade below.
The treatment adopted for the sculpture in the pediments of various
temples may well be made the subject of an extremely interesting
comparison, as great differences are found in such prominent
examples as the Parthenon at Athens, the Temple of Zeus at
Olympia and the Temple at Ægina. In the Temple of Zeus the
figures appear stiff and unnatural, besides being disconnected from
one another, so that they do not arrest the attention or awaken
interest as a group with more action would do. The sculpture in
the pediments of the Temple at Ægina goes to the other extreme ;

the field offered by the cornice hardly seems large enough for the combat which is raging in the tympanum. The Parthenon groups have combined interest and repose—a combination vitally necessary to a great architectural work—in an extraordinary degree.

The Greek was also capable of treating bas-relief in a masterly manner, as is shown in the Panathenaic Frieze, in the Monument of Lysicrates, and in the Erectheion. But while it has far greater scholarship and refinement than the Assyrian, it has not always the vigour observable in the older work. The liberties taken with scale in the Panathenaic Frieze in order to meet the exigencies of subject and position require careful thought before they are adopted in a modern work. At the same time, the relief is—as it should be—essentially an enrichment partaking of the nature of the well-surface below, and is in that respect excellent decoration.

In other instances, as in the Altar of Pergamon, where the effect required is mainly decorative, the sculpture is rightly increased in importance and a much greater relief has been given.

Caryatide figures appear fully developed in Greek art. Those in the Erectheion are beautifully designed for their purpose and admirably carved, so that they do not convey any sense of incongruity. Yet, in spite of its fine qualities, the employment of the human figure for carrying great loads of masonry conveys a somewhat inhuman suggestion, and undoubtedly should only be introduced into a modern design when surrounding circumstances or other points justify its use. This will be further discussed in Chapter III.

By far the most numerous of Greek monuments and perhaps
Monuments. the only form developed into a type is the Stele. Some of these are exceedingly beautiful, and there is no reason why their use should be confined to the tombstone. They may, upon occasion, be introduced into other monumental schemes with good effect. Of monumental work other than the Stele, the best-known is, perhaps, the Choragic monument of Lysicrates. It must be so familiar to all as to need no description.

There is also the Mausoleum of Halicarnassus, of which numerous restorations exist. M. Bernier, of the École des Beaux Arts, has prepared one (Fig. 2), and like the work of all Prix de Rome students, it shows evidence not only of careful study and examination but of a great imagination as well.

M. Pontremoli, also a Prix de Rome student, has restored the
Altar of Pergamon, but in this case it can hardly be said to be

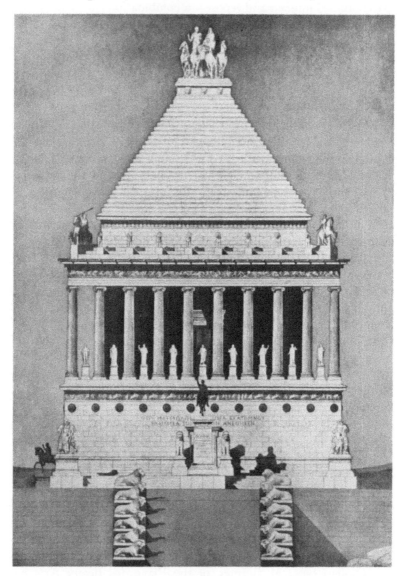

Fig. 2. Restoration of the Mausoleum of Halicarnassus, by M. Bernier.

entirely satisfactory.   Although parts of it are very fine, the
sky-line seems lacking in expression and rather devoid of interest.

The Greek monuments as a whole show variety, interest, imagination and the same scholarship and artistic feeling displayed in other Greek work.   Sculpture in the Greek Period did not as a rule attempt to portray the emotions of the mind.   Its principal aim was the representation of intellectual ideas by the perfection of physical types, and in this field, as in the application of the sculpture to its architectural setting, it stands pre-eminent.

Roman Period, B.C. 272—A.D. 328.

In no period were the national characteristics of a people reflected with more truth than they were in the Art of Rome. The reserve and purity which had governed everything erected in their best period by the Greeks gave way to an ostentation and over-elaboration which increased through the progress of the style until its career was terminated by the transference of the capital of the Empire to Byzantium.   The consequent influx of Eastern ideas which resulted from this change in the seat of government and the action of other forces entirely altered the channels along which Roman Art had previously developed and formed the basis of a new epoch.

In the Roman Period the Entablature was enriched not alone in the frieze but also upon the architrave and the soffit of the cornice, as well as by carving upon the individual members of all three divisions.   The frieze was ornamented in a variety of ways, among which may be mentioned continuous scrolls of foliage, vertical leaves, bulls' heads and garlands, and cupids and garlands, besides the triglyph and metope.

The enrichment of the architrave cannot be considered a successful innovation.   The Greeks recognised that it was a constructional feature and therefore better left to do its work unadorned, but the Romans, in some instances, carved it as elaborately as they did the frieze, with a consequent loss of structural suggestion.   The Temple at Assos in Asia Minor is an example in point.   Here bulls are carved facing each other along its whole length.

The capitals of columns received great variety of treatment. Some have horses, some rams and other animals included in the designs in place of the Greek volute.

The figure found a variety of new positions.   It is used to enrich the apex and the eaves of pediments; the blocks which defined the external stairs of the Temple; upon keystones; and in the spandrils of arches.

In addition to this, special features were sometimes introduced solely for its reception. Thus, in the Forum of Nerva (Fig. 3), a long stretch of blank wall was enriched by means of salient columns supporting a piece of entablature broken around the column, above which was placed a figure. A similar treatment is found in the Arch of Constantine.

The Quadriga as a crowning feature comes into existence.

Fig. 3. The Forum of Nerva. (From a water-colour drawing by Prof. Cockerell.)

Although there are apparently no actual remains in existence, numerous representations upon Roman coins and also in restorations—especially those by Italians of the Renaissance Period—leave little doubt that it was frequently introduced. Its commanding effect and fine decorative outline make it worthy of the admiration it has received.

The brilliant victories of the Roman army in many countries naturally gave great impetus to monumental design, and in Rome were evolved many monumental features which have become prototypes of subsequent work.

Monuments.

Of these, the Arch, by reason of its size, first claims attention. It may be considered under two main divisions:

(1)   Arches with one opening;
(2)   Arches with three openings.

Upon the whole, the single arch is the more successful, and the best of its type the Arch of Titus. The three-opening type is very difficult to handle well, on account of the difference in height of the imposts or the crown of the arch of the small side and the large centre arches. The best known are the Arches of Septimus Severus and of Constantine.

In modern design the American architects have shown that these arches may be introduced not only as monumental works but as an element in the composition of the façade to a large building and a notable example will be found at the Union Station at Washington.

The Victory Column has formed the model for many designs erected in connection with great successes on land or sea. Its cosmopolitan application can be seen by examples in Germany, France, England and other countries. The most famous Roman examples were the Trajan Column and the Antonine Column. The Rostral Column, used to commemorate naval victories, has, however, found few successors in modern work, but its possibilities for design and its variety and interest suggest that upon suitable occasions it might be more frequently used.

It is impossible to exhaust the number of new positions and the versatility of treatment accorded to sculpture by the Romans. Its richness appealed to their love of glorification, and they did not stint its use, albeit they never achieved anything of the perfection of the best periods in Greece, and the Greek work itself had so far fallen that Greek artists were unable to supply work which partook of the qualities of the older sculpture. The etchings of Piranesi should be studied in connection with Roman sculpture and ornament.

Early Christian Period, A.D. 300—604.

The Early Christian Period, for a variety of reasons, possesses practically no remains of sculpture or sculptured decoration of any importance. In the first place, the Christians were not possessed of great wealth, and therefore could not afford to expend money lavishly upon their buildings. Secondly, Paganism was in process of decay, and it was simpler and more economical to transform a heathen temple, with slight alteration, into a Christian meeting-place than to build a new structure. Thirdly, the whole trend of Christianity at this period was against the creation or use of anything which partook of the character of the heathen idol. And lastly, the art of sculpture was at a very low ebb, and it is doubtful if it could have supplied any work of value if it had been called upon to do so.

The work that exists is confined mostly to Sarcophagi, a very few statues, and some carving in ivory upon a small scale.

Byzantine Period, A.D. 330—1453.

The removal of the Capital of the Roman Empire from Rome to Byzantium by Constantine in 330 A.D., gave a new impetus to art by bringing it into contact with Eastern work and surroundings. It received new life, energy and vitality, and developed steadily until about 565 A.D. From 565—717 A.D. the Empire, and con-sequently the art of the Empire, was in a state of decay. From 867—1056 A.D. it experienced a period of revival, then followed the disturbances caused by the Crusades, and practically it ceased altogether with the capture of Constantinople by the Turks.

Similar forces were at work in the Byzantine Period to those already noticed in the Early Christian, so that sculpture, at any rate as far as the figure is concerned, was almost unknown. By reason of the development of the art of mosaic, the ornamentation of buildings by the additions of marble sheathing and also the employment of painting, ample enrichment was at hand, and there was not even any incentive to use sculpture in the round.

Fig. 4 shows the type of decoration employed in Early Christian and Byzantine work.

Romanesque Period, A.D. 1000—c. 1200.

The decay of the Roman Empire was followed by a period of stagnation and barbarism in Europe. Following this came the rise of the Western nations of France and Germany, followed later by that of the Anglo-Saxon.

It was logical that the architecture developed during this period should be built upon the skeleton of ancient Roman work, and in such districts as that of Provence in France, where a number of remains of Roman buildings exist, the classic influence upon both the building and its decoration is found to be most powerful.

The Church was a most important factor at this time, and much of the sculpture was executed in connection with religious edifices, and portrayed incidents and subjects connected with Christianity. It is an undeveloped style and is often grotesque in character. The principal field of ornamentation was in the

Fig. 4. Apse of the Church of San Clemente, Rome.

doorways of the Cathedrals, a notable example being the doorway of St Trophîme at Arles.

In Italy a peculiar feature occurs in the use of lions, supporting the columns of the entrance porch or canopy upon the centre of their backs—a most illogical treatment, which should be rigidly avoided.

Romanesque architecture and sculpture is the foundation upon which afterwards rose the great structure of the Gothic system, and it is in the Gothic Period that fully-developed work is to be found.

Gothic Period, A.D. 1000—1550.

In architecture, the change from the semi-circular to the pointed arch marks the transition from Romanesque to Gothic. In sculpture, no such definite feature exists, but a gradual development leads to the evolution of a distinctive and unmistakable style.

In Italy the influence of classic art is never entirely absent, and sculpture of the Gothic Period did not at any time display the high level of thought, originality and technique shown in the work of the Northern nations of France, Germany and England. Sculpture was employed principally around the entrance doorways to the cathedrals, but some also occurs upon other parts of the west façade. The west end of the cathedral at Siena is a rich example ornamented with a number of statues in niches. In the Doges Palace at Venice figures are placed in niches at the angles of the building, but they cannot be said to have achieved complete success. Sculpture in this position seems somewhat out of place and has a tendency to make the angle appear weak.

In France, the development of ornament and sculpture was much more complete, and the existence of comparatively little ancient work of importance contributed to the growth of a style remarkable for its spontaneity and originality. In the thirteenth century—the best period—the sculpture was in beautiful harmony with its position and surroundings and very decorative in its detail. Later development was towards a more naturalistic rendering, a failing to which French sculpture has always been prone. This desire for realism, which began with a perfectly legitimate anxiety to obtain greater freedom in the expression of thoughts and feelings, ultimately caused the decay of the Art by becoming in itself the goal at which the sculptor aimed. Realistic representation and love of technical skill took the place of the fervour and religious enthusiasm which had inspired the early workers.

As in Italy, so in France, most of the sculpture was connected with religious buildings, and the west end of the cathedral was the principal field for ornament. A line of niches along the whole width of the front, each containing the effigy of a saint, was a favourite feature. Notre Dame at Paris, Rheims Cathedral, and others, furnish good examples. Many of the figures are beautifully carved and show a most artistic rendering of the subject.

Fig. 5.   Doorway of the Cathedral, Rheims.

(*Before the bombardment.*)

The porches, both at the west end and in the transepts, were covered with bas-relief and sculpture in the round. Most of the subjects were intended for the moral instruction of the people, and consisted of scenes representing The Last Judgment, the First Tortures of the Damned, the Entrance of the Blessed into Paradise, the Resurrection of the Dead, and Scenes from the Life of Christ and of the Saints. Saints and martyrs ornamented the piers and arches.

Fig. 6. Doorway of the Cathedral, Chartres.

The porches of most of the principal cathedrals were enriched in this way, and special mention may be made of those at Amiens, Rheims, Chartres (Figs. 5 and 6) and Notre Dame at Paris.

The sculptured ornament in English work was not elaborated to so great an extent as it was in France, and showed a leaning, especially in the early periods, towards the grotesque.

Nevertheless, a great number of excellent figures were employed in some places and impart a feeling of richness and wealth to the façade. Notable among these fronts are those of Wells and

Lichfield, but many possessed carving having a high degree of merit.

Gothic sculpture, although following principles which have little in common with classic work, shows that fitness, precision and complete sympathy with the surrounding forms which marks all truly great periods. The affinity of its detail with architectural shapes can only be fully appreciated after careful examination, but it is then realised how great was the skill and how true the artistic sense that could conventionalise natural forms into such harmonious decorations.

Italian Renaissance, 1377 to present day.

The rise of the Renaissance in Italy, and afterwards in the other countries of Europe, represents a break in the orderly evolution of architecture. Traditional forms were consciously replaced by features taken direct from ancient masterpieces, and these were grafted to buildings designed to meet contemporary needs and circumstances. It follows, therefore, that at the beginning of such an epoch new ornament or a new feature may appear in some instances to be quite incongruous to its surroundings. It is further reasonable to find that the new needs and conditions gave scope for the invention of new forms in which to use these old features.

As Italian Art had never wandered a very great distance from Roman tradition, the Italian Renaissance presents few instances in which a feature obviously belonging to classic architecture has been joined to a Gothic structure. It shows however great imagination and ingenuity in the manner in which these old forms were used in a new type of building, and cannot by any means be stigmatised as a period of mere pedantic copyism.

The dual training of the architects who, during the fifteenth, sixteenth and seventeenth centuries, were often, if not generally, both architects and sculptors at the same time, is a most interesting characteristic of the period. Sometimes they were even masters of painting as well. It follows from this that there is frequently great harmony between the sculpture and its surroundings—an excellent feeling of intimate relationship which is worthy of the highest praise.

In Florence, comparatively little carving was employed, the most noteworthy essays in the plastic art being those of Lucca and Andrea della Robbia, who created the well-known terra cotta ware which has made their names famous.

Both around Rome and around Venice more ornament is found. It was employed in a variety of ways. Keystones of arches were enriched with carved heads, boldly projecting in early work, such as that of Sansovino and Sanmicheli, and with less relief when the broken entablature became customary and the need of the strong centre support no longer existed. The head and bust also appear in this position (Fig. 7), but the majority of such treatments are far from satisfactory. The sculpture seems out of sympathy with the architectural shape to which it is applied.

A favourite enrichment of the spandrils of arches was the medallion carved with a head or group. Three main types exist: one in which the head or group is treated in relief, as in the Ospedale degli Innocenti, Florence (Fig. 17); the second in which the ground behind the head is hollowed out, allowing it to be carved in the round, as in the Palazzo Communale at Brescia (Fig. 18), and the third in which the head is thrust far forward as if leaning through the opening, of which the Sacristy of San Satiro provides a good example. Of these, the type shown at Brescia is generally most effective.

The spandrils are also frequently enriched with figures. These figures show a wide range and variety in their design, from the rather severe and solid work of Sanmicheli at the Palazzo Bevilacqua, Verona, (Fig. 7) to the light and sparkling effect of those in Longhena's design for the Pesaro Palace at Venice. It is worthy of note that each is well in keeping with the work by which it is surrounded, and as such presents an interesting and valuable study. Single figures are used to ornament the sky-line and tops of parapets. In these positions, they often seem rather meaningless, the sharp silhouette obtained by the brightness of the sky behind making an appreciation of any internal modelling impossible, so that the figure depends almost entirely upon its outline for effect. Should this not be very expressive, the result is tame and lifeless. When the figures are backed by the building, the architectural setting forms an admirable contrast and allows greater appreciation of the sculpture. The surroundings of the figures in the Palazzo Valmarana at Vicenza, by Palladio, give them immense value and enable the modelling to be appreciated in a way scarcely possible had they been placed upon the sky-line.

Figures used upon great consoles, as those at the base of the Dome of Santa Maria della Salute at Venice, are most effective and impart quite a picturesque feeling to the building.

Many buildings were ornamented by figures placed in specially-designed niches, and some of these show combinations of fine ornament and good sculpture which are exceedingly beautiful.

Fig. 7. Bay of the Palazzo Bevilacqua, Verona.

One of the best instances is to be found in the Logetta at Venice, by Sansovino (Fig. 8).

Caryatide figures are of fairly frequent occurrence, especially in the later periods. As was mentioned in connection with Greek work and referred to later in Chapter III, these are not always satisfactory. Some of them, however, are undoubtedly not without interest, and two of the most successful are those at the main

Fig. 8.   Niche from the Logetta, Venice.

entrance to the Palazzo Bargellini at Bologna (Fig. 26), by Provaglio. They are excellently modelled, and have a grace and charm which disarm criticism.

The formal garden, although not within the scope of this book, was a most important Renaissance development, and formed an opportunity for the placing of Hermes and Stele heads, besides busts, garden figures and fountains.

Ideal figure sculpture and monumental statuary came into favour, and some fine examples were produced. Two famous equestrian statues are the Colleoni by Verrochio (Fig. 82) and the Gattamalata by Donatello.

Monuments.

German Renaissance, middle of the sixteenth century to the present day.

Germany in the sixteenth century was composed of a number of independent States, and this prevented, to a large extent, any great systematic development of architecture. Nothing of the classical scholarship of Italy is found for a long period, and much of the early work is heavy and uninteresting.

Sculpture occurs principally in the use of symbolic statuary, which was sometimes placed in niches upon the main façade of the building, and the introduction of grotesques of various forms. The grotesques exhibit lively imagination and a certain poetic fancy, but are at the best undeveloped art.

As the style progressed, much of the sculpture became very Rococo, without, however, achieving the brilliant spontaneous cleverness that sometimes makes attractive, work of the corresponding period in France.

In the eighteenth century, Germany experienced a classic "revival," among the leading exponents of which was the architect Shinkel. This revival produced some good work and introduced into the country a purity and refinement which the architecture had not before possessed. Two notable examples which may be mentioned are the Old Museum and the Royal Theatre, both at Berlin. The Brandenburg Gate, which was erected about this time, is a design upon purely Greek lines.

With the modern development of the nation, both architecture and sculpture have advanced very greatly. Much of it exhibits a powerful feeling and breadth of treatment which places it upon a high level. To some extent the influence of "l'art nouveau" is found in fantastic shapes and contorted figures, but this does not seem to have seriously affected the best men.

Some very fine monuments have been erected in recent years, principally in connection with commemorative schemes to Kaiser William I. (See Chapter VIII.)

Monuments.

French Renaissance, beginning of the sixteenth century to the present day.

Early French Renaissance architecture, unlike the Italian, still retained many purely Gothic features. In fact, the structure of many of the buildings was still Gothic and only the decoration showed the classsic tendency. From the time of Louis XIII onwards, however, both sculpture and architecture threw off not only the remains of traditional forms, but also to a large extent Italian influence as well, and both became truly national in feeling.

The best work is brilliant in imagination, versatile in treatment, and has a sense of decoration which makes it pre-eminent in modern decorative sculpture. But latterly there has been a great tendency to lose all structural feeling and to cut and carve stone-work as if it were sugared ornament.

Realism has always been a feature of French sculpture, and where this is kept within bounds it has undoubtedly added to the interest and human appeal of the finished work. It is only when convention is almost entirely abandoned that it becomes so serious a fault.

The use of the carved head is very general throughout the period. It is found upon keystones in great variety, well and harmoniously treated. The carved head has also been used upon console brackets, in medallions, and surrounded by wreaths of bay or oak leaves or branches of palm.

The bust is largely used, sometimes carved separately and placed upon a corbel, as in the Palace at Versailles, sometimes upon a pedestal or in a niche, and in modern work it frequently occurs in the design of monuments to public men. (See Chapter VI.)

The French have executed many excellent bas-reliefs of various forms. Some are wild ungoverned schemes in which all sense of structure is lost. Of this type is the carving over the doorway of the Douane de Rohan, Rouen, which depicts men and horses flying in wild profusion among clouds and other ethereal features. It looks a wild orgy of ornament bursting from the architectural forms by which it is surrounded, but other work is much more restrained and shows great feeling for the limitations of architectural decoration.

The Opera House, Paris (Figs. 9 and 25), perhaps one of the

Fig. 9. The Opera House, Paris.

finest works of modern architecture, is enriched with a great quantity of sculpture, both bas-relief and in the round, the majority being in excellent taste and brilliantly modelled.

The Arc de Triomphe, in the Place l'Étoile (Fig. 98), exhibits a similar richness of feeling; the bas-reliefs by M. Carpeaux show masterly handling in compositions which to the ordinary man would have presented almost insuperable difficulties.

The trophy is a French feature which amounts almost to a new invention. It consists, broadly, of a group of ornament in high relief placed generally near the top of the piers, between the openings of a façade. The front of the Opera House, Paris (Figs. 9 and 25), shows two or three variations of the motif, the group upon the Scaena wall being particularly fine.

Paris and the large cities of France possess a wealth of
Monuments. monuments to military leaders, inventors, artists, poets and statesmen, and their artists have called upon all the forms of classic and Renaissance art to aid them in the work of commemoration. Several of these compositions will be referred to in Chapters VI and VII, and need not be mentioned at length here.

English Renaissance, beginning of the sixteenth century to the present day.

English Renaissance Architecture shows the same grafting of classic forms to Gothic buildings that took place in France, but the isolation of the country and the difficulty experienced in persuading Italian artists to remain in it retarded the development of its architecture and made the style more truly national. Very little sculpture of any note occurs until the time of Sir Christopher Wren, but coupled with or perhaps arising out of the great activity in building at this period there arose a school of craftsmen and sculptors who produced work far in advance of anything previously executed. The vigorous modelling and pleasing attitudes of the figures upon the pediments of St Paul's Cathedral mark them as the production of a master and are characteristic of contemporary work.

It is remarkable, therefore, that a school with so good a foundation should not have handed on its tradition and been the mainspring of a good decorative style. But the fact remains that for a number of years after this sculpture was at a very low ebb.

Firstly with the Greek revival and more particularly from the date of the Great Exhibition of 1851, sculpture, with the other arts, began to revive. Since that time it has shown a steady progression and improvement, and within the last few years has given unmistakable evidence of a great vitality.

Several monuments following classic lines were erected in various parts of the country during the last century.

Monuments.

Of these by far the most numerous were columns, erected principally to the memory of the Duke of Wellington and to Lord Nelson. In London an excellent arch, designed by Decimus Burton, stands at the top of Constitution Hill. There are a number of equestrian and other statues but few of any high degree of merit.

While, possibly, English sculpture may never possess the vitality of that of the French, there is no doubt that the English character should enable her sculptors to produce strong work of definite purpose, both in monumental art and decoration, which may rival the great masterpieces of antiquity.

CHAPTER III

DECORATIVE SCULPTURE

(1) *Intimately related to Architecture*

THE points at which sculpture should be applied to decorate
Points of application. a building require careful consideration. The insistent
nature of the sculpture may be likened to the marks
of emphasis in a musical score. As a melody is sometimes found
running through a more or less florid passage, pointing the whole
composition, so sculpture may be placed, marking the rhythm of
the spacing of the main divisions of the architecture or forming
a continuous band binding the whole together. To use the musical
simile again, a *sforzando* note may occur in such a manner that
it governs a whole passage; in like manner the sculpture may be
introduced where it is the dominant note and forms the focus of
the whole composition of a façade.

Sculpture, therefore, is most appropriately used to emphasise
points which are already architecturally important. If the architectural features are arranged so that they create a composition of
one kind, the sculpture should not attempt to introduce a composition of another. If, for instance, the design consists of two
important pylons connected by a subordinated architectural link,
the pylons should be enriched in preference to the centre portion.
Similarly, the verticality of the shaft of the column should not be
placed in competition with the horizontality of a sculptured band
upon a wall behind, cutting across its centre. If, however, the
band of sculpture be placed at the top, carrying through the lines
of the cap, or at the base, harmony is at once established, because
the horizontal nature of the row of columns is emphasised rather
than the vertical feeling of the single shaft.

Further emphasis is laid upon this use of the bas-relief band
on page 52.

Care should be taken not to add too much sculpture to one sub-
Restraint   division of a building, or there may be danger of the
and profusion.   rest appearing poverty-stricken.   If a large amount of
sculpture grow naturally out of a composition, it will not only be
justifiable, but will be a most commendable feature.   When a more
or less plain wall surface is crowned by an enriched band of
windows, with sculptured panels between, a large amount of sculpture
can be introduced without danger—the sculpture, in this case, being
a logical outcome of the architectural conception.   If, however, the
sculpture in a similar position consist of figures placed on salient
columns, and if it be the only sculpture on the façade, it will very
possibly appear somewhat incongruous.   It is obviously introduced
as decoration, and the spectator feels that it would have been better
nearer the eye, where inspection is easier and there is no necessity
for adding large architectural features for the special use of the
sculpture.

When sculpture is introduced, care should be taken to provide
Contrast.   a plain surface which will act as a foil to the richness
                 of the modelling, and if it is placed in a façade in
which the windows have heavily-moulded mullions and transoms,
many subdivisions, stone-moulded architraves, and possibly columns
and entablatures, it will lose much of its force—the whole surface
becomes so broken that practically no extra value can be obtained
from the modelling.

The sculpture must reflect in design and in detail the spirit
Harmony.   of the adjacent work.   In designing decorative figures
                 or ornament, the sculptor should endeavour to suppress
his own individuality for the time being—or rather, to express it in
the terms used by the architect, for, after all, the fundamentals of
art are universal.   It is only the method of expression that differs.

The principal purpose of decorative sculpture is to ornament
Sculpture   architecture.   When the architecture degenerates into
must decorate   a mere setting or field for decoration, the purpose of
the archi-
tecture.   the building is lost, and with it that governing factor
of fitness which is the key to all great art.   The exact form which
the sculpture enrichment is to take must, of course, depend upon
the individual design, but there are many features which, because
of their frequent occurrence, may well form subjects for consideration and an effort made to discover the laws which govern
their successful use.

B. S.   3

By placing carved heads upon a series of keystones, brilliant
Heads upon keystones. points of interest are created, emphasising the spacing of
the architecture.   If the arcade occur beneath the over-
hanging architrave of an entablature carried upon $\frac{5}{8}$ or $\frac{3}{4}$ columns,
it is frequently necessary to project the head so that it suggests
support in the centre.   If this projection is large, it is very difficult
to bring the head forward in an easy and satisfactory manner.
Perhaps the best treatment is the type found in Sanmicheli's
Palazzo Bevilacqua at Verona (Fig. 7) where the key is formed

Fig. 10.   Keystone, Ritz Hotel, Piccadilly, London.

as a projecting block and the head carved upon it.   If an
attempt is made so to design the head itself that it takes the whole
projection, the probability is that it will become too coarse.   The
Palazzo Pompeii in Verona suffers somewhat in this respect.   There
is no need, in these circumstances, to project the head beyond the
line of the architrave.   If the head falls just behind, it is generally
sufficient.

When a cornice is applied to a wall in such a manner that the
bottom of the bed mould forms the boundary of the arch, much

more freedom of treatment is possible. The head may be shallow or may project boldly. It may have a helmet or some other feature used in conjunction with the head, designed to work back into the architecture above. If a comparatively shallow projection be given, the result is generally better when all the boundaries of the sculpture are made to fall upon the keyblock itself.

Fig. 11.   Keystone, 25–26, Cornhill, London.

The exact treatment adopted must depend upon the surrounding work. If the face of the masonry is rubbed and has channelled or **V**-joints, the female or clean-shaven male head, without too bold a projection, is most suitable, reflecting, as it does, the surface treatment of the stone. If a beard is used it should have a broad treatment that will echo the surroundings as is well instanced in the typically French example from the Ritz Hotel, Piccadilly (Fig. 10).

When the stone-work is hammer-dressed, or vermiculated, or its surface otherwise enriched, then the head may be correspondingly richer and additional features may be added. The beard, under such circumstances, can be made to form a most decorative element,

Fig. 12. Keystone, Strand Front, Somerset House, London.

as also upon suitable occasions can the hair, especially of the female head, drapery around the base of the neck, and the helmet. The latter is often a most useful feature for carrying the carving up over mouldings or other members above and so connecting it to the architecture. The value of beard and hair, both in themselves and also as harmonizing agents, is well seen in the examples from

Nos. 25–26, Cornhill (Fig. 11) and Somerset House (Fig. 12). The great decorative value of palm leaves introduced above the hair is seen in the grotesque head used in the Place Vendôme, Paris. The fine, vigorous lines of the foliage at this point impart an excellent richness to the whole design.

Foliage, especially palm, oak and bay-leaves, may also be introduced below the face, curving up around the head, forming, when thus applied, a most effective frame. The additional

Fig. 13.   Doorway, Pesaro Palace, Venice.

size given is often of advantage in increasing the mass. The head is also a most effective feature when combined with spandril figures tending to maintain a similarity of texture around the arch. An example on bold lines, yet well in sympathy with its surroundings, is seen at the Pesaro Palace, Venice (Fig. 13).

The further the head is projected and the more broken its outline, the more danger there is of disconnection from the architecture, and care must be taken upon this point.

A variation upon the simple head is found in the use of the

The head and bust. head and bust combined—generally a rather unsatisfactory feature. The bust does not lend itself at all easily to the lines of the stonework, and generally it has a very much applied feeling and lack of unity with the structure. Its principal use is in work upon a very large scale, where, if the head were used alone, it would become very coarse in detail. When, however, the general lines of a building are as large as this, it is better to use some other feature. Sanmicheli, in the Italian Renaissance, used the head and bust upon several occasions. One is seen in the ground storey of the Palazzo Bevilacqua (Fig. 7). This suffers in a rather pronounced manner from the detached feeling mentioned above. An example in which the architect has managed to avoid this defect is found in the Porta del Palio, Verona, where the bust is cleverly worked into the bottom of a scroll keystone, and projects boldly under the architrave.

Spandril treatment. The enrichment of the spandril next claims attention. There are two treatments of importance : the Medallion and the Figure. Of these, the Figure may be discussed first.

(a) The Figure. The great factor governing success is to obtain harmony between the architecture and the sculpture. When the arch occurs below the architrave of an entablature, the shadow thrown upon the figure gives it added interest and value, and it may be introduced in such a position with almost assured success. The figure should well fill the shape and be modelled on broad, rich lines, without many dark holes or spots. Such holes will have the effect of breaking up the surface and destroying the value of the complete design.

A rich modern treatment is shown from the Borsig Palace, Berlin (Fig. 14), while Sanmicheli's figures in the Palazzo Bevilacqua, Verona (Fig. 7), suggest a more simple type in harmony with his severe architecture. In the latter instance the somewhat strained attitude and the large amount of plain surface showing beneath are felt to detract from an otherwise satisfactory design.

It is well to observe that in the doorway of the Pesaro Palace (Fig. 13) the treatment is quite opposite in detail to that adopted by Sanmicheli (Fig. 7), but owing to the harmony of the figures with their different environment, satisfaction is still obtained.

The arcade used without an accompanying entablature and

order, but carried upon broad square piers with ample space between the adjacent archivolts, provides a much better space for enrichment than the ordinary spandril ending in a point. A wide base is here provided from which to build up the figure, and a greater sense of structure can be obtained. An excellent example of a composition of this kind is found in the Home Office, Whitehall (Fig. 15), where also the varying relief of the figures produces great richness of effect, and gives increased value to the composition by the variety thereby introduced.

Fig. 14. Spandril, Borsig Palace, Berlin.

The French love of freedom is seen in such a design as the Gare de Lyon, Paris (Fig. 16), where the sculpture, although following the general lines of the spandril, is yet free from any definite boundaries. Such compositions, skilfully handled, are often most effective. The opposite effect is obtained when the spandril is first outlined by a panel and the figure introduced between these enclosing lines. This treatment is inclined to appear hard and unsympathetic, but if the figure is made to cover the space very thoroughly—almost to the point of overflowing its boundaries—

the defect will be largely overcome, and the suggestion of restraint may, upon occasions, be extremely valuable to the composition.

Fig. 15.   Spandril, Home Office, Whitehall, London.

In a medallion treatment there is undoubtedly great difficulty (b) The Me- in creating a design which will establish complete dallion. harmony between the circle of the enrichment and the

Fig. 16. The Gare de Lyon, Paris.

Fig. 17. Arcade of the Ospedale degli Innocenti, Florence.

shape of the spandril. One of the designs illustrated in *Croquis d'Architecture* suggests a combination of a medallion and a palm branch. This is a remarkably successful composition. The medallion is placed in the usual position, while the palm crosses behind it, following in general direction the curve of the adjacent arch. The combination of these two elements promises every possibility of complete success.

The flat circle containing a head or other ornament in low relief, found in the Ospedale degli Innocenti at Florence (Fig. 17),

Fig. 18. Lower part of the Palazzo Communale, Brescia.

is well known. Such a design is only suitable for architecture which has a feeling of great delicacy, and where there is an absence of strong contrasts of light and shade. Often a more harmonious effect can be obtained by hollowing out the circle and cutting the head in high relief or almost in the round. The black shadow emphasising the circle seems to compare more with the shadow throwing up the shape of the opening, than it does with the spandril shape, and there is a consequent gain in the cohesion of the design. The façade of the Palazzo Communale, Brescia (Fig. 18), is treated in this manner, while the plain open circles used in Palladio's Basilica at Vicenza show how valuable is a strong shadow in this position and sometimes the effect of these circles is more successful than the shallow surface treatment of the relief. Contrast and interest may be obtained in some cases by bringing the medallion well away from the wall surface, giving strength, and emphasising the shape by a shadow beneath instead of within the circle.

In a very vigorous façade the head is sometimes modelled as if

Fig. 19. Portion of façade, Royal Institute of Painters in Water Colours, Piccadilly, London.

thrust far through the opening in the medallion. When this is done there is great danger of creating a feeling of restlessness and of disturbing the other lines of the composition. Care is necessary in using such a detail, and it should be limited to positions in which the surrounding architecture compels the use of a somewhat violent feature.

The square panel can never harmonize with the spandril, and cannot in any sense be regarded as a solution of the problem.

The use of the medallion as a feature is not confined to the spandril, but can be employed in several other positions. The most important is the application of a series to a façade—generally, but not always, near the top of the building. Such a series adds great richness to the composition, and emphasises the subdivision in an excellent manner. The contrast of shape to the probable general squareness of the window openings is extremely valuable. A convenient setting is, moreover, provided for busts of famous men connected with the institution represented by the structure. Before it was demolished, the Institution of Civil Engineers in London contained such a feature excellently designed and clearly reflecting the character of the rest of the work.

Medallions elsewhere than in spandrils.

The Royal Institute of Painters in Water-colours, Piccadilly (Fig. 19), has a blank wall relieved by a row of medallions containing busts of famous painters, and this suggests its most appropriate use, viz. upon a building requiring a large expanse of unbroken wall surface and with which a number of distinguished men have at some period been connected. Both the Hôtel de Salm (Fig. 20) and the Opera House in Paris (Fig. 9) show how good a contrast and what great interest is obtained by the use of medallions in somewhat similar positions, and also the necessity of providing an ample amount of plain surface in order that the very different shapes of the various elements contained in the design may not clash.

The attic storey frequently provides an excellent field for the application of sculpture. In any building where it is necessarily deep but has no windows or other openings it may fittingly be carved with a series of panels.

Bas-relief in Panels. (a) In the attic.

Such panels, governed as they are by strong geometric lines, provide a most architectural enrichment. The actual shape of the panel becomes important, but it must also carry through lines already established. Thus, in an attic over a colonnade it is a very reasonable treatment to mark the column by placing above it a figure in the round and by carving the space between as a panel, the alternation of the two providing a variety and contrast which is eminently satisfactory. When so simple a motif is felt to be insufficient, variations may be made upon the theme with great success. Thus the parent treatment (if it may be so called) is found in the New Museum at Antwerp (Fig. 29), while the Opera House in Paris (Fig. 9) provides a magnificent variation. In the latter

Fig. 20. Hôtel de Salm, Paris.

Fig. 21. An Etching from Piranesi.

example the single figure is replaced by a fine group of three figures and a shield over coupled columns and the panel between is a combination of the rectangle and circle, beautifully enriched by appropriate ornament. An etching by Piranesi of a panel showing a combination of a wreath with an eagle (Fig. 21) brings the two shapes into harmony with the ability of a master hand.

Occasionally, several bays of the colonnade are included in one panel, and in such cases it is well in the disposition of the figures, or other elements of the sculptured composition, to recognise the spacing of the bays below.

The frieze may be enriched in a similar manner. In a colonnaded
(*b*) In the
frieze.
front it can be cut up into vertical divisions, either by the classic triglyph or the more modern console, and have the intermediate spaces carved with ornament. Rich sculpture and severe architecture give value to each other, and great interest to the crowning member of the building; the shield and palm of the Palais de Justice, Paris (Fig. 22), is a notably original treatment upon these lines.

The bas-relief panel finds a place also still lower in the building.
(*c*) On the
line of the
caps of
columns.
It may carry on the lines of the caps of the column either by suggestion or in actuality. Such a treatment should only be employed where the shape of the space between the columns is high in proportion to its width, so that after a panel has been formed at the top, the remaining space is still at least $1\frac{1}{2}$ squares high. If the proportion is lower than this, a continuous band, and not a panel, should be used.

The panel is sometimes found at the base of a colonnade.
(*d*) At the
base of a
colonnade.
Here it frequently has the great advantage of being sufficiently close to the spectator for its detail to be appreciated. It is essential, however, that in this position the detail be kept subordinated and refined; if the relief of the sculptured panels be too strong, they will cut across the columns in a most uncomfortable manner, or else look coarse and heavy. St George's Hall, Liverpool, admirably illustrates the value of refinement in the sculpture where the panels at the base of the pilasters are in perfect sympathy with the scholarly architecture, and are themselves well designed and in good proportion.

The bas-relief blocks which ornament the ground storey of the Palais de Justice in Paris, make this portion of the design extremely rich, but they are, perhaps, a trifle heavy compared with the architecture. Although they have not achieved the harmonious delicacy of the Liverpool example they have other excellent qualities of their own.

Fig. 22.   Detail of a portion of the Frieze, Palais de Justice, Paris.

The band of bas-relief panels as a crowning feature can be used *par excellence* upon the astylar front.   Contrasted with the plain sweep of wall surface below, it suddenly bursts forth with strong

(e) To crown an astylar front.

telling notes of high lights and deep shadows fitly governing the whole composition. Generally it has to be combined with windows. If this is done, there are two types of treatment which may be adopted : either the windows may be square and the panels oblong, or the panels square and the windows oblong. As a rule the latter is the more satisfactory.

The Borsig Palace, Berlin (Fig. 23), shows a treatment on the lines of the former. Here the richness of the façade below gives reason to the preponderance of ornament in the frieze.

One other important use remains, and that is the employment

(f) To change a motif.

of the panel to carry on the lines of a feature already established, but to change the motif. Used for this purpose it may give added interest to the centre part of a composition, and an admirable example is seen in the Hôtel de Salm, Paris (Fig. 20). Here the change from the simplicity of the architectural pediment to the vitality of the sculpture is a masterly stroke, and combined with the dome and the standing figures above the cornice, gives good expression to the rotunda and completes its command over the whole façade.

On the other hand, comparative repose may be suggested when the space in the centre bay between impost and cornice is occupied by a great arch, but in the side bays by the carved panel. Under these circumstances its office is to maintain the lines of the architecture in a strong yet unostentatious manner, and in order to do this it follows that sculpture of too virile a nature should not be used.

The Arc de Triomphe in Paris (Fig. 98) well exemplifies the point, the broad band of simple mouldings admirably fitting the sculpture for its office.

In some positions the strongly marked enclosing lines of the

Bas-relief in bands.

panels are undesirable features, and a better effect can be produced by their elimination—the relief running through in a continuous band. In buildings which have a large wall surface without strongly marked vertical lines, this is particularly noticeable ; under these circumstances the bas-relief combined with mouldings at top and bottom becomes a strong binding force sufficiently powerful to dominate the mass. Generally speaking, the sculpture should not be given much relief. If it is brought too

Fig. 23. Façade of the Borsig Palace, Berlin.

far away from the wall there is a danger of disconnection by producing a big contrast without any transition from one to the other. The Panathenaic frieze is famous for the perfect unity that has been achieved between sculpture and architecture and its excellent qualities need no reiteration. The Athenaeum Club, Pall Mall (Fig. 34), is a scholarly example of the Greek revival, while the

Fig. 24. The Albert Hall, London.

Albert Hall (Fig. 24) executed in terra cotta of two colours upon a flat surface suggests a type of treatment worthy of further consideration.

The excellent combination and proportion of surfaces in the fragment from Piranesi (Fig. 75) is worthy of close study, the added relief here being well in sympathy with the general richness and decorative qualities of the design.

A repeated similarity or a logical sequence of shapes in the

detail is a necessity in order to produce the flow of line upon which the success of the bas-relief band depends.

The danger of setting up competition between the sculptured band and a row of columns has been referred to previously, but if the line of the top of the band is continued around the columns, and the base of the shaft is carved with bas-relief, all the dangers of such a feature are obviated and an effect of the greatest richness is produced.

This continuation of the band around the columns is impossible when it is placed in the middle of their height, and it should never be so employed unless other portions of the design react upon it and prevent the disastrous results referred to above.

If the band is placed just below the cap it is sometimes successful, although a series of bas-relief panels are generally more satisfactory in this position.

Free sculptured ornament used upon a building may be at The trophy. times not only perfectly justifiable but most appropriate. A group of this kind carved above a large plain surface often gives immense value to both itself and the architecture around, providing furthermore an opportunity for the display of design of the highest order, and the use of symbolic objects having relation to the purpose of the building. The wall of the theatre may have a trophy of masks and musical instruments or that of the Naval College of a ship's prow with anchors lanterns and ropes, in each case appropriately reflecting the occupation of the user of the structure. The success of free design of this kind depends upon the artistic feeling of the designer, and if it is not skilfully done is apt to look foreign to its position. When the sculptured ornament is governed by architectural forms, as the ornament upon the piers of the ground storey of the Opera House, Paris (Fig. 9), the relation of the trophy to the general proportions of the design may be more certainly defined than when it is arranged in a purely arbitrary manner. With proper architectonic feeling however, an excellent effect may sometimes be produced.

The magnificent eagle and shield on the Scaena Wall of the Opera House (Fig. 25) is a splendid conception for its position. It seems to have achieved a feeling purely sculpturesque without sacrificing in the least due subordination to the surrounding architecture and is worthy of the highest praise.

Appropriate positions for the trophy are at the heads of the piers of an astylar front where they become crowning features

Fig. 25. The Angle of the Scaena Wall at the Opera House, Paris.

corresponding to the capital of the column. Similar positions near the angles of buildings emphasising the main outlines of the

structure, or on the ground storey under the platt band are equally
good placing.

The supporting figure in any form should be regarded as

most dangerous. Upon occasions it may be, and undoubtedly has been successful, but the mere idea of
a human being condemned to carry enormous loads of
masonry for all eternity must be somewhat revolting to the human
mind. It is no argument to say that the figure is in stone, or is
not altogether human, the fact is suggested and the association
of the carved figure with the normal human being will always
be conveyed. Such an objection becomes aggravated when the
figure is placed in a physically-impossible position, curling around
under a three storey oriel window, or attached by some extraordinary but invisible means to a wall surface; neither attitude
nor position seems logical, and although Art may upon occasions transgress beyond the line of human limitations, yet it
should always have a very apparent reason for doing so, or else
the transgression must be a transgression in fact only, and not in
appearance.

The most marked exception to the objection raised against
supporting or Caryatide figures is of course the Atlas. Atlas is a
well established myth conveying a definite association to every
mind and, as such, may be very reasonably employed.

The entrance door to the Palazzo Bargellini (Fig. 26) is an
instance of a very skilful use of the figure supporting a light load
and it is not in this instance very offensive. The actual modelling
may account for some of its good qualities and the scale and
relation of the doorway to the whole façade give it value as
decoration. The attitude of the figures suggests strength and
refinement and they appear to a certain extent to carry the load
without effort and with grace and dignity.

In the ordinary way the Caryatide is unsuitable for a palace
or for a residence of any description, but when the purpose of the
building is light and to some extent frivolous, its use becomes a
possibility. The whole building is in playful mood and strict
adherence to the demands of fact is not expected.

When a theatre, music hall, or similar building is under consideration, a treatment of this kind is permissible, but as suggested
above the figure should be treated as if the load was not in the
least irksome and the load itself should be apparently easy to

Fig. 26.   Entrance doorway, Palazzo Bargellini, Bologna.

carry. A possible position is under the cantilevers of the glass
awning. The very lightness of the material makes the weight seem
negligible. There remains one other possible variation, and that is
the carving of a figure which in mass and detail seems a very giant
of strength, capable of supporting any weight which could possibly
be placed upon it.

Such a suggestion is conveyed by the upper part of the
torso and head, employed at the Germania Insurance Office,
Berlin.

Possible exceptions have been noted. It is reasonable to
suppose that there may be others, but as a rule the Caryatide, or
any figure supporting a vast load should be avoided.

The classic pediment provides a great field for the display of
Figures in a   sculpture, but one presenting immense difficulties to
pediment.   the design of a really satisfactory and cohesive group.
The shape, running from an absolute point to a comparatively great
height, has caused solutions to be attempted on various lines. The
one which, perhaps, promises most success is that which involves
the creation of a common point of interest. By this means,
cohesion at least can be obtained. By raising the centre figure
upon a block, a scale less than the largest possible is used and so
undue cramping at the angles is prevented. The alteration in the
attitude necessary for the grouping is familiar to all.

The Royal Exchange, London, shows a peculiarity in so far
that the figures are all in a more or less vertical position. They
are not so unsatisfactory as might be imagined, but undoubtedly
lose connection with each other to a large extent.

Another variation, not often attempted, is the use of bas-relief.
Most of the difficulties connected with the filling of the space are
by this means obviated and a large amount of interest can undoubtedly be obtained. Many subjects also lend themselves to
such a treatment. The richness of the full figure is missed without,
perhaps, a sufficiently tangible gain in other directions. Examples
will be found in the West Front of St Paul's Cathedral, and at the
Mansion House, London.

The small pediment, especially when curved, does not present
nearly the same difficulty, but no great amount of variety of attitude
is possible. The detail, of course, can always be varied. It should
be borne in mind that the composition will need some centre feature
or focal point. Where such is not employed the general design

½ INCH DETAIL

Fig. 27. Design for the Entrance to a Block of Municipal Offices.

will lack cohesion; generally, figures seated back to back are employed, with some object of a more or less architectural nature between. The Opera House, Paris (Fig. 9), will again provide an example. The lines of the shield are possibly not quite satisfactory, but the general composition admirably fulfils its purpose, and is in good harmony with the rest of the design.

The main entrance-door to a building is a most appropriate position in which to add enrichment. Here is to be found a wide field for design, depending upon the individuality of architect and sculptor. The sculpture, should, however, be so designed that it is not merely an adjunct but a distinct element in the composition of the door. It may be placed either above the general architectural lines, or enclosed by them ; in either case it must have intimate and obvious connection. The group of figures above a carved or sloping pediment is a common feature. In many instances the figures convey the impression that they are in danger of sliding off. This could be obviated by placing blocks of stone at the angles in the nature of the Greek acroteria, thus giving the figure a square seating. The lines of the sculpture should not flow in the same direction as the sloping architectural forms, but return into them, suggesting a counteracting line which would be found of great value. The overhanging of limbs at the ends is generally a mistake.

Enrichment of doorways.

The probable prototype is to be found in Michael Angelo's figures on the Medici tombs, but while such a feature may be quite permissible upon a tomb, upon a building having more severe lines and definite purpose, it is apt to strike a false note.

The interest of a certain amount of freedom in grouping can sometimes be used with advantage, provided that care be taken to enclose the sculpture within architectural boundaries. The introduction of the American eagle over the doorway of the Soldiers' and Sailors' Memorial, New York (Fig. 107), is very cleverly handled in this respect. In the author's design for the entrance doorway to a block of Municipal Buildings in a seaport town (Fig. 27) a large group of sculpturesque form is kept in restraint by the architectural line around. Symbolism is introduced by using Viking Boys, the prow of the Roman Rostra, and other naval accessories to suggest the value of foreign commerce and the highway of the sea to the prosperity of the town and its close connection with ships and shipping.

The French, with their usual exuberance, use upon occasion a wild splash of ornament over the doorhead, contained often within architectural boundaries it is true, but otherwise taking enormous liberties with material and surroundings. An instance of this is seen in the doorway of the Douane de Rohan at Rouen, where every license is given to the sculpture. Although such work may at first sight seem attractive, it is most unsound and upon closer examination will cease to seem in good taste. Quite unstructural and indeed unarchitectural in treatment, it must inevitably lead to decadence.

CHAPTER IV

DECORATIVE SCULPTURE

(2) *Applied*

WHEN there are no restricting conditions such as cost or speed
Haphazard of construction, a strong temptation is felt by the
application. architect to introduce fine groups of sculpture into
his compositions quite irrespective of their fitness. Sometimes a
generous donor will present such a group, and expect that a place
will be found for its use.

Whether due to these or other causes, sculpture is frequently
seen that has every appearance of being an afterthought or of having
been introduced for a purely arbitrary reason without any relation
to the surrounding architecture, except the relation of physical fact.

Sculpture with haphazard placing ought never to be allowed
upon a building. Unless it is a necessary element in the design
from its first conception, and a logical production of its development, it has no place in the structure.

Proper atmosphere is as necessary to the display of the
Atmosphere. sculptured group used as a decorative feature as it
is to a studio work. For this reason there should
be no suggestion that its position is confined, or that there is too
great a preponderance of plain surface around.

Groups which occur upon the sky-line will have great influence
Sky-line upon the final effect. Often they almost govern the
sculpture whole composition. They should, if carefully placed,
express the principal masses and general disposition of the parts.
This is one of their chief uses, and properly applied, they will
become powerful agents towards the attainment of so desirable
an end.

The modelled group is always an important element in a
The value of façade, and its importance will be vastly increased
bronze. if the material is changed from stone to bronze. By
reason of this contrast, even greater care is necessary to obtain

perfect relation between the mass of the sculpture and the disposition of the planes of the surrounding architecture than is the case with a group executed in stone.

The silhouette of the single figure used upon the sky-line is of the utmost importance. In fact, it is hardly too much to say that its whole value as a piece of decoration will depend upon the amount of expression which can be imparted to its outline. Very little of the half-tones or internal modelling of these figures can be seen, owing to the glare of the sky, and if the outline does not express the action, such figures look more like dolls than representations of the human form.

The single figure upon the sky-line.

The figures upon Pennethorne's fine front of the Civil Service Commission in Burlington Gardens (Fig. 28), lay themselves open to this criticism. Their attitudes, especially when viewed from the front, lack expression, and the influence of time and weather have not improved them in this respect.

If figures in such a position can be provided with a background, or even partially screened, they will gain immensely. Such an effect will be obtained from a roof rising behind the balustrade. The roof slope is a great factor in the success of the well-known figures in Palladio's Basilica at Vicenza. If to the value of the roof be added the interest of a building curved in plan, the figure becomes a most successful terminal feature, for when placed around a semi-circle or a portion of a rotunda every figure is presented to the spectator at a different angle, and interest is thus well maintained. Such a treatment is found in the Hôtel de Salm, Paris (Fig. 20), where the whole centre portion is treated as an enriched and important domed feature. When forming part of a purely decorative colonnade, a large number of figures may be justifiable, but when they are used in vast profusion upon a utilitarian structure they become purposeless, vain repetition without result. A comparison of Bernini's colonnade at St Peter, Rome, and the New Palace at Potsdam will show the truth of this contention.

A large amount of action is not always a necessity. Frequently figures in simple attitudes will give sufficient effect for the purpose. In the Gare du Nord at Paris (Fig. 32), for instance, the lines of the pilasters require suggestion above the cornice, but need no further accentuation, and the simple action of these figures is sufficient to do this. More

Action.

action or any great variety would have been fatal to the required
effect. As it is, they are excellent crowning features. In other

Fig. 28. The Civil Service Commission, Burlington Gardens, London.

instances, where they form part of a sky-line composition, acting
as connecting links between more massive groups at the ends and
centre, something of the same sort is required, and in this case, the

more unostentatious they are made, the more efficiently do they fulfil their purpose.

If the figures are few or widely-spaced, they should be well clothed and given some definite action which will enable them to overcome their similarity to a block of masonry crowned by a sphere which is generally taken to represent the head. In these cases drapery is very necessary and very expressive, and upon that account the female figure may often be applied with much greater advantage than the male. If the male be used, it should have a cloak or some substitute for drapery to give it the necessary mass.

Care must be taken to prevent a feeling of disconnection of the figure from its base; it should never merely stand upon the balustrade—specially-designed blocks should always be provided for its reception.

When the standing figure is brought below the sky-line it falls
The single figure below the sky-line.
(a) Standing.
more naturally into the decoration of the building, and the absence of a sharply-defined silhouette allows the internal modelling to be more readily appreciated. It still remains, however, a very brilliant piece of ornament, and may be used with excellent effect, for example, in an attic treatment over a colonnade in conjunction with bas-relief panels. The figures well sustain the importance of the column that marks the spacing of the bays, and their combination with the panels forms an effective band of enrichment. A good example of this is found in the New Museum at Antwerp (Fig. 29), where also the figure is brought well into view by being raised upon a block over the cornice. The end pylons of the composition define the boundaries of the ornament in a most satisfactory manner, and are rightly left without sculpture of any kind. Such a contrasting surface immensely increases the value of the enrichment and should always be provided—its ornamentation will not, as might be supposed, add to the effect, but will cause the whole surface to have the same tone value—a comparatively uninteresting grey.

If, on the other hand, the figure is placed against a vast expanse of plain wall surface, in all probability so violent a contrast is created that the figure seems absolutely foreign to its position, or else the background appears ill-considered and incomplete.

The further the figure is brought away from its background,

Fig. 29. The New Museum, Antwerp.

the greater amount of atmosphere it obtains. There is then, however, some danger that it may appear disconnected. The

Fig. 30. Angle Pavilion of the Houses of Parliament, Berlin.

angle of observation, also, will throw it against other features further along the façade, and if these are much broken in detail their lines will have a most disagreeable effect upon the sculpture.

B. S.   5

When the placing is on a salient column or similar feature, the connection of an architectural blocking course will generally be sufficient.

Fig. 31.   Agricultural Building, Omaha Exhibition.

This can be seen in the angle pavilion from the Houses of Parliament, Berlin (Fig. 30).   If this example be compared with that from the Agricultural Building, Omaha Exhibition (Fig. 31), the value of the

connecting block in the first example is at once apparent. In the
Exhibition Building, however, the attic rising above the sight-line

Fig. 32. The Gare du Nord, Paris.

of the heads of the figures, and the treatment of simple panels upon
the attic wall which are high enough to act as a background, gives
much more sympathy between the sculpture and the architecture

5—2

than is found in the horizontal mouldings and broken surfaces upon
the Berlin example.

Almost all the decorative effect of the terminal figure upon the
sky-line is obtained if it is used over a screen in front of the main

Fig. 33. The Entrance, Law Courts, Antwerp.

façade of a building, and many of its defects are eliminated. Here,
as noted in the examples above, it is essential that the architecture
behind should be treated in a restrained and simple manner, and it
is further important that the figure is not seen partly against the

architecture and partly against the sky from any point of view. The Louvre furnishes an example which is not open to criticism upon any of these points.

A framework of architecture around any sculpture is extremely valuable, and when the scale of the building is sufficiently large, figures may be employed to decorate individual features in a most successful manner. Such a treatment as that of the figures over the small columns of the Gare du Nord, Paris (Fig. 32), enclosed by a great semi-circular arch, is most effective. The setting, the

Fig. 34. Athenaeum Club, Waterloo Place, London.

background, and the contrast are alike good and suggest an excellent motif for future work. The Law Courts at Antwerp (Fig. 33) show the figure used in a manner frequently to be found in that city, and its combination with the arch of the main entrance gives dignity and importance to the design.

When used upon a large scale as a focal point, the figure may give distinction to a whole façade. When so used, sculptured ornament should be employed elsewhere upon the building to echo the rich spot of the single figure, otherwise it will appear foreign to its position.

Fig. 35. Figure of "Sculpture" from the Grand Palais, Paris.

The harmony between the central figure and the structure behind is excellently obtained in the front of the Athenaeum Club, Pall Mall (Fig. 34), and its position in the centre of the façade, both vertically and horizontally, gives it the necessary importance.

Contrast between the figure and the column is nearly always successful, especially if the column is fluted. Richness is produced in a totally different manner in each case, and enables the two features to be combined with harmony and without fear of competition.

The value of a combination of the two features can be appreciated in the detail of one of the figures used in the centre part of the main elevation of the Grand Palais, Paris (Fig. 35).

The tall and slender form of the standing figure has not sufficient mass for use in some positions and in these cases the seated figure becomes more suitable. The end of the podium wall in an approach designed upon the lines of the front of the Roman Temple is a case in point. The strong square outline of such a group at either end of the long horizontal lines of an approach of steps well defines the boundaries of the composition. If the architecture of the façade behind is treated upon broad lines either as a plain wall surface or as a colonnade, it will add greatly to the value of the sculpture. These two elements in combination are found in the Bureau of the American Republic, Washington (Fig. 36), where also additional value is given to the sculpture by raising it above the eye-line.

The single figure below the sky-line.
(b) Seated.

Where the design of the structure calls for their use, figures in pairs guarding an entrance will be just as effective as is the single central group in front of a pylon. The most vital point is to provide them with an ample and adequate base and to connect them in a logical manner to their surroundings. It is not sufficient simply to provide the space necessary for the sculpture, there must be atmosphere and breadth to avoid any possible tendency to meanness.

The Federal Court House and Post Office, Indianapolis (Fig. 37), is a case in point. Its simple harmonious and imposing lines are well worthy of study.

The seated figure gains an admirable contrast if used at the base of a great plain surface. Sufficient enrichment should be

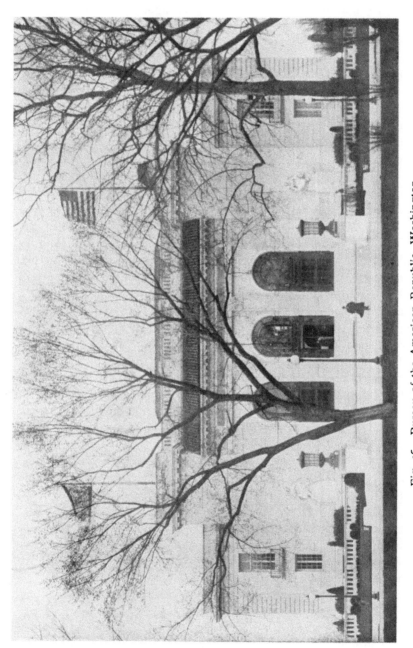

Fig. 36. Bureau of the American Republic, Washington.

given to prevent the sculpture from appearing foreign to its
position, but no more, and the figure left alone to display its
sparkling beauty without the distraction of competing lines. The
base of a tower or the end pylon of a composition which is not
disturbed by window openings may be treated so that it is suitable
for the reception of such a figure. Sir Aston Webb, in the
Admiralty Arch, Pall Mall, has recently shown how successful this
treatment may be, and similar use is made of the figure in the Pont
Alexandre III Bridge in Paris (Fig. 38). In the latter case the

Fig. 37. Federal Court House and Post Office, Indianapolis.

whole composition is of a most decorative character but sufficient
contrast is maintained to give the sculpture its true value.

As a terminal feature above a colonnade or screen, the seated
figure is not so often used. It practically necessitates a wide base,
which neither the ordinary column nor the pier will give. Occasions
arise, however, when either coupled columns or columns and piers
present a width of surface which the single standing figure could
not successfully terminate. The seated figure may then be most
useful. The careful arrangement of drapery in such circumstances
will enable it to meet any reasonable requirements.

Reference may again be made to the Civil Service Commission, Burlington Gardens (Fig. 28), where the single seated figure has

Fig. 38. Pylon to the Alexandre III Bridge, Paris.

been most appropriately used well in sympathy with the architecture beneath.

Highly decorative compositions call for the special employment
Figures in　　of the figure, and provision must be made for its recep-
niches.　　tion.　It is thus that the niche is introduced.

When so employed, it should be an obviously logical treatment, anything which suggests crowding or the cramping of the figure by the architectural surroundings will ruin the final effect. In many instances of the use of this feature the Renaissance architects were eminently successful. The figures of Sansovino in the Logetta at Venice (Fig. 8), or those in St Maria degli Angeli at Rome, are a standing witness to the enormous value of one controlling mind for all the details of a feature involving great qualities of design in each of the two Arts.

While it may hardly be possible to obtain such complete harmony in modern work—architecture and sculpture having each a separate exponent—the architect can at least place his niche in such a manner that it will be in harmony with the rest of the façade. The enrichment of the first floor of the Borsig Palace, Berlin (Fig. 23), by niches between the windows, is a well-thought-out example. The entire absence of mouldings around the niche prevents competition with the window openings and also maintains the unity between the ornament and the adjacent masonry. It would have been fatal to have attempted elaborate architecture in such a position.

Where the design of a façade involves the use of end pavilions without window openings, the pavilions can be effectively treated with a series of figures in niches carrying through the lines of the fenestration in the centre portion of the building; if that portion is treated with a colonnade, the niche will be even more effective. In any case, the rich yet solid masonry, broken in certain places by so virulent a feature, will be extremely valuable to the whole design.

The niche, like the single figure, gains immensely by contrast with the column. If used in a colonnade, however, it should not invariably be employed in every inter-columniation. In many cases if its use is confined to every other bay or to certain well-marked divisions its value will be enhanced by the reserve displayed in its application.

The use of the niche isolating the figure suggests that it should be used in a position which will allow the sculpture to be easily examined. It should not be placed high up on a building. Its more reasonable use is upon a ground or first storey. The figures in Pennethorne's Civil Service Commission building (Fig. 28) are very satisfactory in this respect, and are also admirably connected to the architecture.

When, however, the whole façade has a large amount of ornamentation and niches are employed in the lower part, it is quite

Fig. 39.   Tower of the Palais de Justice, Brussels.

logical to continue them above, although it may be impossible to examine the figures upon the upper stories.   Such a use as found in the Home Office, Whitehall, for instance, is quite reasonable. The only criticism here is that in comparison with the large heads in medallions over the windows, the scale of the figures is felt to be somewhat small.

It is necessary, in a tower or an architectural composition of a
similar nature designed with several tiers placed one
above another, to aim at a pyramidal effect, and to
prevent monotony a variation in shape is frequently
desirable.   Where such change occurs the two parts

The figure at the transition from one form to another.

are liable to appear disjointed and the figure will, as a rule, solve
the difficulty of connection in an easier and more satisfactory
manner than any architectural feature.

If a circular drum is placed upon a square base, the figure can
be designed to fill the void created by the difference in the two
shapes.   The junction must not then be slurred over and the figure
left to perform its office as best it may.   The sculpture should be
recognised in the treatment of the angle, and the angle made into
an important feature.   The sculpture should also receive recognition in the circular drum above.   By this means the whole design
can be connected into a unified group.

The dome of the Palais de Justice in Brussels (Fig. 39), is
an example of a beautifully harmonious transition.
Observe how the salient columns crowned with small
bronze griffins echo the figures above, carrying the con-

The Transition figure used seated.

nection of colour down into the building.   The break in the ring of
columns and the small projecting portico shows that the sculpture is
as much part of the architecture above as it is of that beneath, and by
setting the figure upon a high block, the sag which would otherwise
occur at this point in the suggested line is prevented.   The contrast between white stone and bronze and the reflection of the
bronze colour in the copper dome complete one of the most satisfactory pieces of grouping to be found in modern work.

The tower over the offices of the London and Lancashire
Insurance Company in Pall Mall (Fig. 40) is treated in a
peculiarly English manner.   The transition is here from a square
tower to an octagonal turret by means of an intermediate storey
square on plan but having hollow angles, the hollow passing later
into the splay.   By raising a block upon the front and dropping
the figures, the architect has brought the two portions of his design
closely into touch with each other, so that the upper part seems a
natural growth from the lower.   The broad treatment of the drapery
is quite in harmony with the general squareness of the massing.

The seated figure in this position is more common than the
standing, but the latter is sometimes found when there is a strong

verticality in the architecture.   The tower of the Rathaus in Char-

lottenburg is treated in this manner.   It is a charac-
teristically German type of composition, the general
lines rising boldly and square some distance above the
ridge of the lower roof, then the figures occur, and the upper part
is set back, while the top is formed with a peculiar shape somewhat

Fig. 40.   Tower of the London and Lancashire Fire Insurance Office,
Pall Mall, London.

in the lines of a lantern.   The latter feature is not very pleasing,
but the standing figures at the angles are quite good.

The approach to a building needs accentuation.   The building
must be joined to its surroundings and become part of
a larger whole ; it cannot be called successful if it jumps
suddenly out of the ground without any preparation.

Various expedients are employed in different places to soften the transition. Perhaps the most usual and useful expedient is the flight of external steps. The single figure used to define the end boundaries of such a feature has already been mentioned, but when the architecture is very massive or particularly large, the single figure is not sufficiently commanding, and some group form must be employed. The same feeling should be reflected in steps, pedestal and sculpture.

Thus, should the steps be long and low, then a low pedestal and low type of grouping is most in sympathy, and will give good results. If, however, the general mass of the steps is comparatively

Fig. 41. New County Hall, Glamorgan, showing sculpture groups.

high, the figure and the pedestal beneath should correspond. The shape of the pedestal and of the lines enclosing the group should be similar in proportion and also, generally, in size. An interesting comparison will be found between the sculpture used at the Glamorgan County Hall, Cardiff (Figs. 41 and 42), and the magnificent groups upon Shinkel's façade to the Old Museum at Berlin (Fig. 43). Thus, in two very different types of building a most successful and harmonious treatment has been found.

The exact opposite to large groups such as these is found in the small Hermes. Generally it should not be used close to a building, but if a terrace or drive intervene, then it will fulfil its office of emphasising the boundaries

Small groups on approaches.

in a very efficient manner. Occasionally it is used in a city building at the entrance to the forecourt, and such a treatment is found in the École des Beaux Arts, Paris; but the heads, in this instance, seem to be rather large in scale for their position.

Many other treatments for sculpture groups upon approaches will suggest themselves. The dominating quality must be an intense

Fig. 42. New County Hall, Glamorgan, showing sculpture groups.

sympathy—sympathy of form, sympathy of design—and if that is achieved the result must be harmonious, arresting and full of interest.

The terminal group upon the sky-line, like the single figure, Groups on depends almost entirely upon its silhouette for ex-the sky-line. pression.

The whole value of both mass and interest must be obtained from the outline; the detail within this boundary will add nothing but the necessary richness. To help towards this end, wings, limbs,

Fig. 43. Detail of Group in front of the Old Museum, Berlin.

or portions of the drapery may stand out in sharp silhouette against the sky, breaking away from the tame outline of the figure in repose. Variety of mass is necessary, and some sort of triangulation in the arrangement of the group is advisable in order to provide a substantial base.

Some of the most successful groups in this position are those upon the Opera House, Paris (Fig. 9). The central standing figure holding aloft a lyre, with two seated attendants, on the apex of the Scaena Wall, and the groups over the end blocks of the front, are excellent in expression and vitality, and the interest they give to the sky-line would be difficult to surpass.

While vigour is needed and worth some sacrifice to obtain, care must be taken that the outline is not too broken and violent. Interest is necessary, but restlessness must be avoided.

From the days when the chariot race in the circus was arranged for the entertainment of the Caesar and the people, and the chariot was an element in the more fearful pastime of actual warfare, it has always possessed a magnetic attraction for the human mind. When to this attraction is added its immense value as a decorative feature, it is small wonder that there are many occasions upon which it has been employed. Fortunately, it has been fully recognised that miniature quadrigas or like features are a misapplication of the motive, and they have been avoided. This has necessitated the reservation of the quadriga for large and important structures which are of a scale suitable for so important a crowning group.

The quadriga.

A certain amount of spirited action is invaluable, but this should not degenerate into mere violence. The restlessness of any group of sculpture apparently flying from its position into space will always make it foreign to the logical lines of architecture.

The quadrigas on the angles of the Grand Palais in Paris, are badly at fault on this point. They create an impression by the marvellous skill and dexterity displayed in both modelling and fixing and not by beauty of line or good qualities of massing. Thoughtful study of such groups must lead to the conclusion that excellence of design is more important than excellence of technique, and success in the one must not be confused with the attainment of the other.

The rich outline of the quadriga may receive added qualities from the employment of certain adjuncts.

In the Kaiser Monument, Berlin (Fig. 103), distinction and majesty have been added to the quadrigas representing North and South Germany by the addition of great standards to the figure in the chariot. A small boy in front of the quadriga in the Wellington Arch, Constitution Hill (Fig. 97), gives a naïve touch in an unexpected position. When the horse quadriga is too broken in outline for the surrounding design, the substitution of lions for

Fig. 44. The Municipal Theatre, Frankfort.

horses will give a bold and simple effect, retaining still plenty of richness and vigour. Such a group used to excellent advantage in the Municipal Theatre, Frankfort (Fig. 44), is well placed in the centre of the composition and enclosed by the architectural features.

The massive outline of a stone group maintains the squareness of composition characteristic of masonry shapes, and its use instead of the customary bronze may sometimes be more appropriate and harmonious. The distinctive shapes given to the Town Theatre,

6—2

Dortmund (Fig. 45), whether in agreement with English ideas or not, will be seen to possess a strength and value which could not have been obtained with any other treatment.

When the powerful effect of the quadriga is too great the biga becomes a useful feature. It can give to the sky-line enormous value, especially if used in conjunction with a similar group at opposite ends of a building. Such a composition

The biga.

Fig. 45. The Town Theatre, Dortmund.

is that of the New Museum at Antwerp (Fig. 29). The horses appear, perhaps, a little thin, the sharp contrast of bronze and bright sky tends to give this effect more where only two horses are used than when the value of four can be obtained. The figure, also, perched above the chariot looks a little disconnected. Apart from these points the groups combine with the rest of the composition to produce a most satisfactory whole.

Care must be taken to avoid the danger of so many different

shapes becoming disconnected from each other. If the base is too great and the designer attempts to spread the group it may lose its cohesion and with that much of its force.

In certain instances the equestrian figure is more suitable than
The eques-   the biga as a terminal feature. A pair of such figures
trian figure.   may be placed in a position like that just discussed, or
a single feature can be made effective in a central position. Supporting figures are sometimes added, giving increased interest and greater mass. The drapery of these figures next to the base of the group is a great advantage, supplying weight at a point where it is most needed, yet which, with the horse used alone, is very difficult to obtain.

A group somewhat upon these lines is used in the centre of the Houses of Parliament, Berlin.

The silhouette of the horse, either with or without wings, or
The horse.   accompanied by an attendant figure, and the griffin,
will frequently be found of great value at the ends of a pedimented front. Often also a horizontal sky-line receives great invigoration by the introduction of such a feature. An examination of the sky-line of the Scaena Wall of the Opera House, Paris (Fig. 9), and of the Old Museum, Berlin (Fig. 47), will show the value of its use in two situations quite distinct from each other.

The eagle and the seated lion are suitable forms for use as
The eagle   terminal features, while in special buildings, such as
and other ani-   are found in Zoological Gardens, other animal forms
mal forms.   may find decorative employment. The main consideration is that they should have a distinctive outline and possess decorative qualities. The camel is effectively used to crown a pier at the Zoological Gardens, Antwerp.

The large sculpture group opens up an unlimited range of
Large sculp-   possibilities in design. Its use must naturally be
ture groups.   reserved for occasions upon which there is ample
room for its display and reason for its use. It is always essential, however, that it should be placed well above the eye-line of the spectator.

Failure to observe this condition is the only thing which prevents the complete success of the fine groups in front of the Museum of Painting and Sculpture, Brussels (Fig. 46), they are otherwise very satisfactory and interesting. The groups at the Opera House, Paris (Fig. 9), are practically free from this defect due largely to the fact that the whole building is raised upon a broad flight of steps.

The groups upon the Arc de Triomphe, Paris (Fig. 98), must be regarded as great compositions. The immense difficulties of satisfactorily grouping figures in two tiers have been overcome in a masterly manner. The marvellous dexterity which is here displayed cannot however be given unqualified praise.

Fig. 46. The Museum of Painting and Sculpture, Brussels.

The practical English mind asks for something of a more logical and reasonable nature, something which will have an appearance of physical possibility. In endeavouring to satisfy this feeling probably some of the emotional effect now present would be lost, but upon the other hand the group would gain in structural qualities and in that repose which is an invariable characteristic of a great work.

CHAPTER V

THE PLACING AND SURROUNDINGS OF MONUMENTS

WHEN a monument assumes great importance in the public
mind its location is generally the cause of an extraordinary amount of discussion. It is a common
experience to find that a large number of sites which
have the most diverse qualities are suggested, and eventually, after
the waste of much valuable time, energy and labour, abandoned as
unsuitable or inconvenient.

The
question of
location.

Useless discussion, like all wasted labour, is much to be
deplored. A large proportion of it might in many cases be
avoided if a few more or less necessary requirements were laid
down and all sites not possessing any of them refused consideration.
As it is, the proposed positions are not brought forward upon any
special basis. The majority simply represent a certain amount of
unoccupied ground which the proposer, from personal interest,
personal association, or a desire for notoriety considers it worth
while to bring before the notice of the committee.

No system is worthy of more severe condemnation. It results
in caprice or chance, sometimes even sheer desperation, ultimately
deciding the fate of the proposed group, and it is eventually found
in a situation which could not be more incongruous. When there
are no recognised lines upon which a decision can be made, it is
not difficult to understand why this should sometimes be the case.
The committee is often composed of men having great educational,
clerical or political abilities, but no special training to fit them for
the work in hand. They are presented with a heterogeneous
collection of schemes and suggestions and often before, as well as
after they have completed their deliberations they are subjected to
the most scathing criticism in the public press. Finally a decision
is made to locate the proposed monument, not in the situation

which they themselves consider the best, but in the one which seems to offer the least opportunity for adverse attack.

When a site is found in close proximity to a building so that it partakes as it were, of the same atmosphere, the statue should be erected to a man whose life and work were intimately connected with the structure or with the institution which that structure represents. The connection should preferably be personal, not one merely of chance, or of social position.

Connection of the work of the man with the building.

Richard I for instance, was head of the English Realm and as such connected with her government, but he, perhaps, of all kings had least to do with her actual home affairs, and his position under the shadow of the House of Commons has no justification. The mere fact that the peculiar contour of the road offered sufficient room for the placing of the pedestal without unduly hampering the traffic is no argument at all.

Oliver Cromwell, on the other hand, a man whose whole power and intellect were concentrated upon obtaining proper rights and representation for the people, is justly honoured by a place beneath walls within which those privileges are now discussed; but his statue, unfortunately, owing to the exigencies of the site, has been dropped into a ditch. He has certainly obtained recognition in the right position, but at what a cost!

The connection between monuments of men, and the buildings with which they were associated, need not be confined to single statues, but could be considerably extended.

The connection of great men with appropriate buildings.

The approach to an Art Gallery, for instance, might well be enriched by a scheme of lay-out involving a number of sculptured figures representing great artists of the past.

The association between the men and the building in such a case would be perfectly natural, and one which would add considerably to the interest of the immediate vicinity both to the casual visitor and to the Art student.

Imagine what enhanced value would be given to the courtyard of a palace, if representations recalling the famous kings and brilliant courtiers who had once trodden its paths or rolled in luxurious carriages over its cobble paving, formed features in its adornment.

Schemes such as these could be designed in their entirety and carried into execution as circumstances demanded or occasion arose, just as a hall may be panelled for enrichment with painted frescoes to be added one by one until the whole is complete.

The location of statues and monuments in streets should be controlled by similar laws to those which govern placing in connection with buildings. The reservation may be added that unless there is some strong reason to the contrary, the lives of certain men make their commemoration unsuitable amidst the prosaic surroundings of street architecture.

Location of monuments in streets.

The painter, the sculptor, the poet, or the musician, have no part in the artificiality, the stress and the hurry of commercial life. They are better in the public garden or in the park, although when, as will occasionally happen, their work has been largely connected with a particular locality, commemoration in that locality is logical and just. The politician, the philanthropist, the civic dignitary, or even perchance the architect, might be fittingly surrounded by the things for which they laboured.

The market-place, the centre and the hub of local life in a country town, is above all places the situation for the famous man who was once a native of that town.

Location in a market-place.

The broad square gives the monument dignity and importance and by association the worthy citizen of to-day is constantly reminded of the noble example of his predecessor.

Likewise the city square, or the public " Place," suggests a setting for the heroes of a larger sphere. The great generals of the army and admirals of the fleet, whose pluck and skill have won for the nation the proud position which it now enjoys, who have gained for its inhabitants security and peace, should stand in their midst.

In a city square,

The business man hurrying about his daily work and the more leisurely seeker after pleasure pause for a moment and pay homage to the man, remembering that by his sacrifice they themselves are richer and more honoured than they would have been had he preferred a life of lazy luxury and indolence in the safe keeping of his home.

The public garden is a constant resort of many toilers of the city, who wend their way here to pass a few leisure moments snatched from the weary round of work. It may, therefore, well harbour the statues of great men whose

In a public garden.

lives and labour connected with Art, Music, or Religion had a great influence upon the lives of their fellows, recalling the great benefits they have bestowed upon the age in which they lived.

The surroundings are, moreover, in sympathy with the outlook of such a man during his lifetime. He would in all probability have found delight in these quiet precincts and would have loved to wander in its paths or linger under the shadow of its trees, musing upon the marvellous current of humanity flowing by.

It is a delightful thought to associate the Embankment Gardens with the memories of men such as Robert Raikes, founder of Sunday schools, or Sir Arthur Sullivan, whose music has provided hours of happiness to thousands of his fellow workers.

There is no incongruity in the close proximity of the two men. Each had a sphere of activity widely removed from the other, it is true, but their work is more or less universal and will appeal to broad-minded men as having a distinct and definite value which is none the less real because of the divergency of its aims.

It is probably necessary upon this point to use some discrimination. There may be occasions when to place monuments close together of men who had widely different ideals, would lead to a situation bordering on the ridiculous.

To place for instance, a man famous for preaching the abolition of war, next to one of our most brilliant generals would hardly appear a happy selection of the respective sites.

The park has at least two groups of monuments suited to its environment. One, by its association with the realm
In a park.
of Nature to the memory of exponents of the Arts has been previously mentioned. The other is for those monuments which by their great importance require an adequate setting to obtain proper expression—such a setting as it would be almost impossible to obtain in the confined areas of the town.

These monuments, robbed of suitable surroundings, cannot ever receive reasonable appreciation or proper value. Their size, and the large number of points of interest which they contain, require leisure for their examination, the help of distance and atmosphere to merge them into one coherent whole and these are only to be found where ample space is available. If the Albert Memorial (Fig. 108) could be transplanted into a city square no larger than the area covered by the bottom block of steps, it would occupy an unjustifiable amount of space, and after the sacrifice had been made the composition could never be appreciated and the detail of the grouping only very imperfectly realised.

Association is an important factor in the human character, and it ought not to be so flagrantly ignored as it is upon many occasions. When its demands are reasonably met the gain to the completed group, the added force of the story which the monument has to tell, is out of all proportion to the extra difficulty involved in obtaining a site to meet the requirements necessary in each individual case.

The importance of association.

As with a decorative group, so a monument placed close in front of a building will re-act upon the structure, and conversely, the architectural lines of the building will have an important effect upon the monument. It may be well to consider this point in detail.

Monuments in close proximity to buildings.

If the ground storey of the building contains large circular-headed or other openings, the statue may be so placed that it is framed by the black shadow of the void behind, gaining at once a most appropriate setting. Some of this effect will be lost if the statue is of bronze; it is, therefore, in such cases better kept in stone or marble. The effect will also be most unhappy if portions of the design project beyond the boundaries of the opening when viewed from the most important standpoint. The group, under these circumstances, should be designed so that it recognises and obtains full value from the opening behind.

If the architecture is particularly strong and expressive it may throw the sculpture entirely out of scale unless great care be taken to prevent it from so doing.

In this connection may be mentioned the sculpture in front of St George's Hall, Liverpool, which is contrasted with architecture upon a magnificent scale, with the strong lines of a splendid colonnade. Here the sculpture fails entirely to maintain the high artistic level of its surroundings.

The Kaiser Frederick Monument, Berlin, seen in conjunction with the Old Museum (Fig. 47) preserves the scale of the building much more satisfactorily, although the detail of the design of the pedestal may be open to criticism.

Care should be taken that the effect of sculpture in front of a building is not ruined by the forecourt railings. When the building faces a roadway, but is set some distance back from the frontage line, it frequently happens that the guard railings are continued straight across the front. When a monument is designed to stand in the space so enclosed, the top rail and vertical spike of the ironwork may cut right across the lines of the sculpture, so that it is impossible to gain an adequate view of the whole group. Viewed from outside the railings interfere, and inside the spectator is too close for proper observation. Under such circumstances, either the monument should be incorporated in the design of the forecourt screen, or else the screen should be so designed that it recognises the monument and allows it adequate expression.

Fig. 47. The Old Museum and Kaiser Frederick Monument, Berlin.

The incorporation of the monument in the forecourt wall has been most successfully effected in the Étienne Marcel Statue in Paris (Fig. 48). This equestrian group, placed upon a high pedestal, is in excellent relation to its surroundings. Its elevation above the roadway gives it power and a commanding aspect, while the architectural base appears a most natural growth from the masonry of the balustrade. The architecture of the Hôtel de Ville behind is strong enough in scale and treatment not to suffer by contrast with so vigorous a feature.

The horse looks away from the building, as it obviously must; but there sometimes arise occasions when doubt apparently exists as to the direction in which it should be placed. The one or two examples of horses facing towards the structure are quite sufficient to place the point beyond dispute. When it faces inwards, the confinement of the outlook, the absurdity of elevating a man far above the ground only to limit his horizon by a flat wall surface

Fig. 48. The Statue of Étienne Marcel and the Balustrade of the
Hôtel de Ville, Paris.

comparatively only a few feet from his horse's head, is sufficient to condemn it at once.

The sculpture group may be placed so that it carries through the line of one portion of a building which sets forward from another.

This may be done by using a balustrade projecting some distance from each side wall towards the centre as part of the boundary of the courtyard and placing sculptured figures at the termination

Fig. 49. The Pont au Change and the Place Châtelet, Paris.

so that they mark the boundaries of the opening through which the building is to be approached. Or a single monument may stand in the centre while the building forms a semi-circle behind. This latter placing may be seen at the Place de L'Institut, and a similar impression is conveyed at the Place Châtelet and the Pont au Change, Paris (Fig. 49). The Institute has a bridge approach upon its central axis; the monumental figure is placed upon this line and forms an admirable contrast to the architecture of the façade, while it creates quite enough suggestion of enclosure to prevent the forecourt space from having the appearance of a formless void. In the Place Châtelet the shape of the monument gives great effect to the buildings behind, and its own interest is greatly enhanced by the surrounding foliage.

Where the front of the building embraces a large flight of steps the monument may sometimes be combined with them with excellent result. If there is sufficient room, the block forming the base may be placed in the centre of the flight; this is sometimes satisfactory. Unless, however, it is very carefully worked the monument is liable to have the appearance of an encumbrance. Its use should be reserved for occasions when such a treatment is the only one possible.

When a wide landing intervenes between the top of the steps and the building, the monument, if placed upon the space, will have a commanding position. The great difficulty to be overcome, if the flight be very lofty, will be occasioned by the sight-line of the front edge of the landing cutting off the view of the group. This may be largely obviated by the use of a lofty pedestal, or it can be considerably reduced by the introduction of a landing half-way down the flight, making the spectator at the bottom some distance away from the base of the statue, and correspondingly lowering the angle of sight; the use of wide treads and shallow risers will be in a similar manner of additional benefit.

The design of the external stairs to the National Gallery, Berlin (Fig. 50), shows an equestrian statue very successfully incorporated with the actual structure. Stairs start up at right angles to the main axis and the flights return upon themselves somewhat in the manner of a dog-legged stair, and the statue is placed upon the main axis above the top balustrade. The building behind has a colonnaded front which forms an admirable foil and the placing of the whole group is a most spontaneous and even brilliant conception.

The satisfactory result achieved by placing a group in front of a colonnade has been emphasised in the Chapter upon Applied Groups of Decorative Sculpture, pages 71 and 73.

No attempt should ever be made to divorce a statue from an adjacent building. When such a placing is adopted the contrary idea must be paramount and no effort spared to create an intimate relation between the two.

The indiscriminate placing of many street monuments con-
Monuments tributes very largely to the lack of appreciation which
in streets. they frequently receive. No monument should ever

Fig. 50.   The National Gallery, Berlin.

be placed in a thoroughfare unless there be adequate reason for its presence. The reason must spring from a definite and obvious source, and is better if of an architectural rather than of a sentimental character, although if both can be procured the site will possess qualities which approach the ideal.

Many monuments along one street, especially if the street is sufficiently straight for several of them to be seen at once, create a bad impression. Their very multiplicity detracts from their value and their probable variety of shape and size will suggest a heterogeneous collection having no definite relation or purpose.

The simplest placing for a street monument is to be found at a simple break in the building-line of the thoroughfare where there are no cross-roads or other special features in the road itself. Such a position may have points to recommend it. If the scenery and buildings suddenly brought into view are pleasant, and the break is not so large as to amount to a gap, the probability is that a well-designed group will be successful.

The monument to Naval Cadets at Brussels (Figs. 51 and 74),

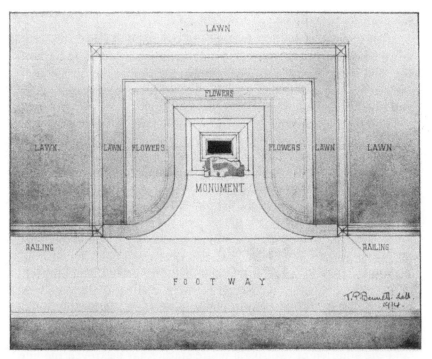

Fig. 51. Plan of the Monument to the Naval Cadets, Brussels.

for instance, has a most charming effect. A broad avenue rising up a hill is bordered by fine trees and massive houses. Near the top a glimpse is suddenly obtained of the Palais de Justice, and in front of this a monument of beautiful form and colour, ranging from a pale grey to brilliant white, bursts into view. The surrounding ground is further laid out with a colour combination, comprising yellow calceolarias, pink geraniums, light grey-green and also red leaved plants. The whole composition is most satisfactory and full of life and interest.

B. S.   7

The street junction at the side of a main thoroughfare frequently provides a site for a monument. The most common defect of this situation is the narrowness of the side street, which does not provide adequate room for the base, there being a tendency for the final effect to be somewhat crowded. Atmosphere will often be gained by setting the group slightly back from the frontage-line of the buildings. By this means an additional feeling of enclosure is obtained which is very valuable, and it also ensures the provision of a field of architecture as a background when the group is seen by a spectator approaching from the side.

If the angles of the side road naturally expand at this point, great advantage will be gained. Not only in this case does the form of the road suggest provision for a monument, but by the diversion of the traffic into a broader path it necessarily becomes less dense and gives freedom and access to the sculpture.

The placing of a monument in what, for want of a better term, may be called a back-water of a busy thoroughfare, is full of fine possibilities and excellent points. The comparative quietness entices the pedestrian to turn aside and examine the work. Its proximity to a main artery of the city ensures its publicity, so that it has the advantage and the help of two most opposite elements in its due appreciation.

Such a position as that of the monuments in Waterloo Place before the recent alterations (Fig. 52) gives additional value to the sculpture. It is also certain that the sculpture helps the expression of the thoroughfare. The Regent Street end of Waterloo Place without the Crimea group would appear very bare, the traffic would seem scattered, and the street lose the very definite lines of direction which it has at present. The re-siting of this monument and the addition of two single figure statues has destroyed the fine sense of scale and simplicity of placing which existed previously. The old lay out is here referred to in all cases.

The intersection of two roads provides another possible site. Generally speaking, it is better if one of the roads is definitely more important. If three branches are important the monument can be designed to present an interesting side to each and in that case the unimportant branch will with great advantage be utilised for the back of the figure. The statue must have a back, and in a single figure this is extremely uninteresting.

An equestrian figure would have a good effect in this position.

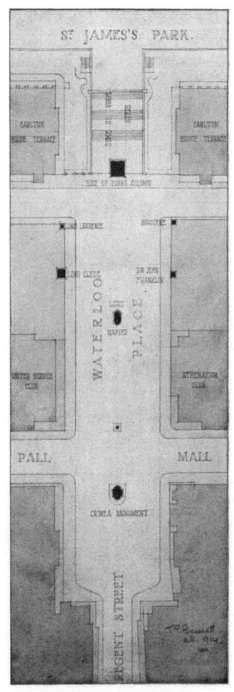

Fig. 52. Plan of Waterloo Place, London.

The front and the two sides always provide good points of view, and this ensures that at least the majority of vistas can receive consideration.

For single standing figures the Teniers (Fig. 67) and Quinten Matsys (Figs. 53 and 69) monuments in Antwerp have almost ideal situations. They are both approached by wide roads upon the front, and have thoroughfares approaching upon two sides only slightly less important. The back street leads directly to the park. They are thus framed with the verdure of trees and surrounded by the scholarship of architecture. The park of itself is obviously a back, and so does not call for special treatment.

The intersection of many roads often leaves a comparatively wide open space which is avariciously appropriated for a monument. It does not always offer so many advantages as would appear at first sight.

The irregular nature of the site makes a really harmonious shape extremely difficult to obtain, and the various angles from which an important view is required do not simplify the problem. Furthermore, the architecture of the surroundings will not, in all probability, form any definite series of lines which can be utilised as a frame, and from many points the monument will be seen partly against a building, partly against the sharp perspective of a street-front—even, possibly, against the sky, showing through at its termination. This parti-colouring in the background is one of the worst conditions against which the sculptor could possibly have to contend, and every effort should be made to prevent its occurrence.

There are some street junctions which suggest solutions of the difficulty. If two roads enter at a wide angle, and the building-line on this side represents the base of a triangle whose apex is the point of intersection, this triangular space will offer a situation possessing many good qualities. The flat frontage-line behind will offer a reasonable setting and the direction of the lines enclosing the monument emphasise the importance of the principal point of view. The actual angle and number of the remaining roads is of comparatively small moment, except that it is an advantage to have them converging upon the centre-line of the group. Frequently the recognition of a certain proportion of the roads will produce a more satisfactory result than a placing which makes concession to a number. Generally the square or the circle in such places will be the best foundation upon which to build, and the same shape

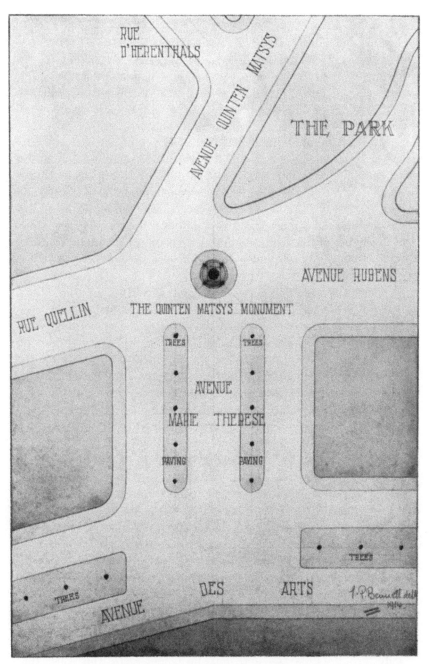

Fig. 53. Plan of Streets around the Quinten Matsys Statue, Antwerp.

should be kept throughout the height. If the upper part is designed upon the circle and the base upon some other figure, the alteration will emphasise the regularity of the monument to the detriment of its surroundings, and with a loss to the whole. The simplicity of one definite form is the least disturbing element which can be introduced where the units of the surrounding work are disposed in such a way that they display marked irregularity.

Many of the most important thoroughfares of continental cities have fine gardens down the centre, which offer an environment for the monumental group impossible to obtain upon this side of the Channel. Not only is excellent atmosphere given to the work, but space is obtained for proper observation, and the addition of the soft qualities of colour in flowers and verdure close to the more severe shapes of the sculpture and the hard lines of the surrounding architecture combine all the elements necessary for a successful composition.

There are many examples of such a setting as this. The Armand Steurs (Fig. 71) in Brussels, can be quoted as one type. Here a wide avenue is planned having a green space lined with trees down its centre, and near the end of the thoroughfare an important cross-road intersects. At this point, and behind the intersection of the road, is placed the group, so that it can be viewed from its best aspect by a spectator anywhere in the open centre space; subsidiary view-points are obtained at the sides, and owing to a change in the direction of the road behind, the back is largely screened.

A second type is found in the treatment of the roadway in front of the National Bank, Antwerp (Fig. 54). The centre feature consists of a large fountain of rather uninteresting, though heavily-ornamented design; at some little distance upon either side are groups of sculpture. Here they are merely decorative groups, but the situation would answer equally well for a monument. The bronze is placed upon a plain block of granite which obtains excellent expression from a raised plateau of lawn, upon which it is set. The proportion of the various parts of this scheme is particularly good, the relation of sculpture, lawn and flowers to each other being most harmonious.

A third suggestion is found from the arrangement of the Franz Laure group (Figs. 55 and 80) in Ghent. In this case the garden lay-out is along the centre of a minor street connecting two

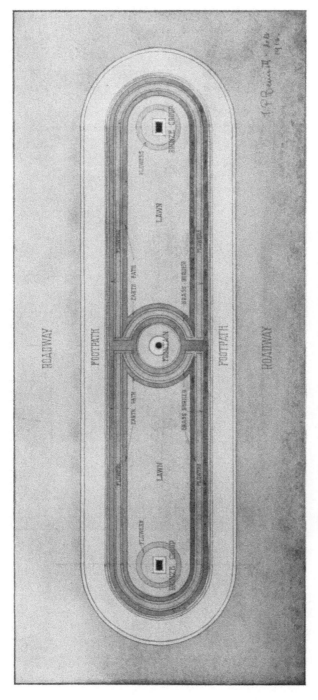

Fig. 54. Plan of Garden in front of the National Bank, Antwerp.

main thoroughfares. The monument, which is of a somewhat
unique type, is recessed sufficiently from the road towards which it
is made to face to allow a semi-circular space planted with flowers
to be arranged in front. By virtue of the wall-like form given
to the setting of the bas-relief, it forms a satisfactory enclosure to
this space. The green at the back is planted with two rows of

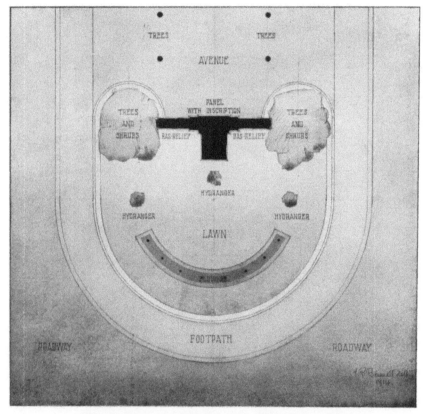

Fig. 55. Plan of the Franz Laure Monument, Ghent.

trees, and a bronze tablet and inscription behind the stone screen
containing the principal relief, sufficiently recognises the scheme of
lay-out adopted for the avenue.

The road junction site may range from a small space formed of
the intersection of two or three streets to the great
city place. When its size increases to a large extent,
the open space and amount of sky visible between the

The town
square and
city place.

buildings becomes proportionately much greater and the monument will have its silhouette emphasised in a similar manner to that pointed out as a necessary accompaniment of the single figure placed upon the sky-line of a building. If, in such circumstances, the group is to form an important factor, it will have to be of great magnitude and capable of maintaining its individuality against the various forces which will be found in competition. Monuments in large irregular spaces, like those in small indefinite crossings, are best designed upon the simple shapes of the square and the circle.

As a rule, the designer should no longer attempt to be subservient to roads and the voids in the buildings, but should make his group the nucleus around which the whole interest of the locality will centre.

The Monument de la République in Paris (Fig. 88) is eminently successful because its size and the force of its design become compelling factors rivetting the attention, and the ragged edges and raw ends of streets and turnings pass unnoticed.

To drop down a small equestrian figure, or a single sculptured group in such a situation, is absolutely courting failure, they could never be made to appear other than mere street refuges enriched with a rather unusual amount of ornamentation.

When, however, the outline of the place becomes regular and provides a geometric setting, a scale is at once created which must govern everything that finds a place within its boundaries. The variety of treatment possible in these large places has no limit. The parent of them all is the market square. Generally without pavement or obstruction over its centre it forms a wide field thronged upon market day with all the inhabitants of the country-side.

The sentiment attached to such a situation is alone sufficient ground for its choice as a site for the commemoration of the great names of the locality; and the aesthetic value of its wide and unobstructed area could hardly be surpassed. It is preferable, if possible, though not a vital necessity, that the design of a monument for such a position should possess a certain magnitude.

The smaller square opening from the side of a main thoroughfare can frequently be made the site of a monumental group. Such squares are not necessarily kept free from obstructions and are frequently planted with trees, providing an item of interest that is a considerable asset. The appearance of these squares, viewed from a busy thoroughfare thronged with people, is most inviting, creating as it does a contrast between the heat and dust of the road and the broad shadows of the trees, and when sculpture is introduced as an additional attraction the picture presented approaches near to perfection.

The Place Stevin in Bruges (Fig. 56) presents such a picture, and a short time spent lingering in one of the cafés found at the side of its shady precincts, and studying the statue in the centre will long remain a most delightful memory.

This type of square is capable of considerable extension and is not necessarily confined to the small provincial town. The important city street may find a similar adjunct upon a larger scale of inestimable advantage. Here, of course, the lay-out must follow more formal lines. The planting, instead of encroaching upon the centre space, is better kept at the sides (unless it is arranged in a very formal manner), but the square may well be used for more than one statue. If this be done, each statue should form part of a large general scheme—the individual group being connected by design and in subject to the rest, and certain groups made to dominate the others. The old arrangement of Waterloo Place (Fig. 52) possesses many of these points, but the subjects of the various groups lack connection, and very little value is obtained from the four statues placed at the sides. Otherwise the relative scale of the various parts is well maintained. The commanding form of the Duke of York's Column (Fig. 94) seen against the open park, the suggestion of enclosure of the important yet subordinated mass of the Crimea Memorial, and the smaller monument to Lord Napier, form the most important group, and additional interest is well given by the four pedestals mentioned above. The place is felt to be well furnished yet not crowded, and the effect of the whole lay-out is more than satisfactory.

From the subsidiary place it is easy to pass to the consideration of the central place.

Here formality and enclosure are essentials. When the scheme is large and intended for the placing of a number of groups, these must be arranged in an orderly manner. George Square, Glasgow, is completely ruined by the neglect of this principle.

Trafalgar Square, London, has many excellent points which often pass unnoticed. The arrangement of the retaining walls, steps and balustrade in front of the National Gallery, and the pedestals for equestrian figures at either end are admirably planned

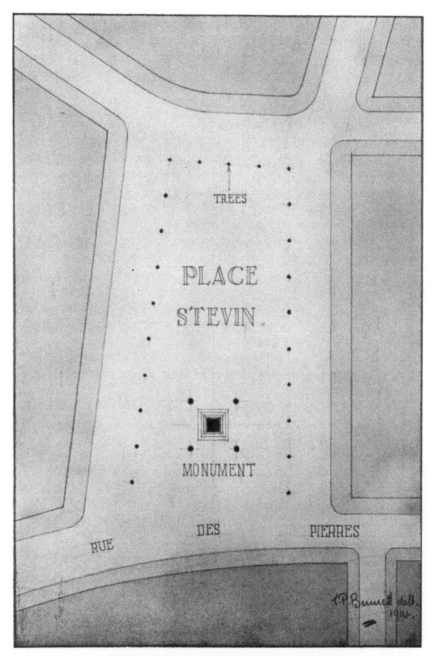

TREES

PLACE

STEVIN.

MONUMENT

RUE   DES   PIERRES

Fig. 56. Plan of the Place Stevin, Bruges.

(see Fig. 84), and the relation between the Column (in spite of the somewhat unfortunate design of its base) and the statues of General Napier and Sir Henry Havelock, connected by a link of granite posts, is particularly good.   The wide and irregular spacing of the various roads and their entrances partly contributes to the difficulty of proper appreciation.

The opposite to this loose definition of the site is to be found in the restricted lines of squares having few openings arranged in a plainly formal manner.   One of the simplest, and at the same time one of the most satisfactory, is the Place Vendôme, in Paris.   The enclosure of the central column by the lines of the surrounding buildings seems to give it more expression than it receives in almost any other position.   It takes away from the somewhat lonely effect which such a feature sometimes has.   The single axial road gives ample expression and seems to emphasise the value of the column.

When a place is planned upon a rectangle having an important road passing through upon its longer axis, and another entering on the short axis opposite an important building, the centre will form an excellent site for an equestrian statue.   The arrangement of the roads is such that the three good views of the monument are on important vistas, and the fourth side, from which very little effect can be gained, is shut off by the building.

This can be readily appreciated in the placing of the statue of Godefroid de Bouillon in Brussels (Fig. 83) and an examination of the square and approaches should leave the conviction that it would always, with the help of good design, be a successful arrangement.

Even more enclosed than the Place Vendôme is the very much smaller space known as Exchange Flags, in Liverpool, where a square space without roads for vehicular traffic is, except for small openings for entrance and exit, entirely surrounded by buildings. This becomes little more than a courtyard, and the laws governing placing in close proximity to buildings are more applicable than those for open squares or places.

Finally, an example may be given in which the monument forms the *raison d'être* of the whole lay-out.

The Place Lambermont in Antwerp (Fig. 57) is selected. The relation of shapes on plan is particularly well managed, and the use of water in the centre gives great additional interest.   A fault may be found with the sky-line.   When every feature has the

Fig. 57. Place Lambermont, Antwerp.

stamp of formality, a broken roof-line such as is found here is very unhappy. It has been blocked out in the illustration, because it is very difficult to realise the beauty of the sculpture from a photograph when the eye is worried by the broken effect of the roofs at the top. The reproduction as it stands really portrays the result which would be obtained if this defect had been avoided.

By the public garden, as here discussed, is meant a small garden lay-out, generally of a formal nature, found in the hearts of towns—a refreshing oasis of green amid dusty roads and uncompromising masonry.

The public garden.

These gardens, by virtue of their situation, are generally somewhat confined in area, and if a monument is placed within their boundaries it should be made the nucleus of the whole design. The paths should lead up to and round about the statue, and the arrangement of lawn and flowers must assist in its expression. When the garden is the central feature of a square, having approaches upon its sides not on the axial line, it is better to surround the garden with bushes high enough to form a screened enclosure and confine the range of effect of the monument to persons within. When, however, the square and the garden it contains are set back from a thoroughfare and connected by a short cross-road, the sculpture group can be seen from the more important street and should be transformed into an important feature closing that vista. The trees and bushes around should be designed to help this expression and to compose a background.

In such an instance as in Russell Square, Bloomsbury, where the enjoyment of the garden is reserved for the privileged tenants of the surrounding houses, the statue is much better placed on the boundary of the garden and the axis of the approaching road, for the enjoyment and appreciation of all who may pass by, rather than in the centre of the square, where it could only be seen by a comparatively few.

Where the garden is on the border of a road it may sometimes be advisable to raise the monument well above the surrounding level and to make it face towards the thoroughfare so that it can be seen by the ordinary traveller along the highway. Under these circumstances, there must be no forced suggestion. The monument must be brought naturally into prominence, or the effect will be disastrous. When several groups are contained within the same boundary they should be designed as part of one scheme, the relative importance of the various units determined and maintained, and a certain similarity of feeling carried through the whole.   In the groups of the Embankment Gardens this fault is felt.   None of

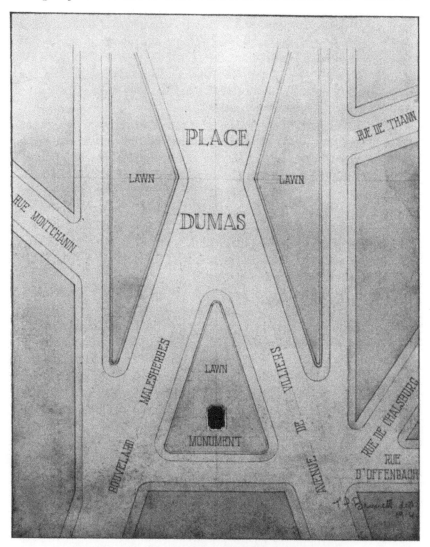

Fig. 58. Plan of a portion of the Place Dumas, Paris.

them bear any relation to each other in size, placing or design, except that they are made to line, and there is no doubt that the individual group as well as the general effect, suffers in consequence.

Where the garden is not defined by roads but by buildings, the monument should be connected in placing with the buildings. It may in this way suggest enclosures in a most delightful manner.

The Gambetta Monument in Paris (Fig. 91) effects this excellently. The Louvre sets back, forming three sides of a rectangular space appropriated to a garden. Across the front of this space there runs a road leading out into the lower end of the Rue de Rivoli. The placing of the Gambetta defines this roadway in the centre, and gives its direction and situation an emphasis which it could not possibly otherwise obtain.

The Place Dumas, Paris, is another most effective arrangement (Fig. 58). Here roads converge in front of the monument, cross each other and open out at the far end, enclosing, placed apex to apex, two triangles. In the centre of the base of each is placed a monument—at one end Alexandre Dumas Père, and at the other Alexandre Dumas Fils. The seated figure of Dumas Père faces inwards towards Dumas Fils, and the back of this monument, past which there runs an important road, is handled in a most masterly manner by a transposition of the points of interest (Fig. 59). This will be again referred to in Chapter VII.

The informality of the park and the possibility of providing,

The park. within bounds, any necessary arrangement of surroundings, is frequently of inestimable advantage. The backs, and sometimes the sides, of groups are comparatively uninteresting, and the use of trees and bushes to prevent the spectator from obtaining a view in an unfavourable position is a point worth consideration. The contrast of colour to be obtained between a background of trees and a marble group is very valuable, and the advantage of preventing too close an approach by the use of flower-beds and lawns should not be ignored.

The diverging paths upon either side of the Guy de Maupassant group (Figs. 60 and 62) give room for a very satisfactory placing, the freedom of the surroundings gives it atmosphere, and it obtains a most satisfactory silhouette from its fine background of trees.

When the monument employed is of a particularly distinctive shape, the surrounding park-land should be laid out specially for its reception. Thus, if it consist of a form based upon the semicircle, it should have an axial approach, and its back should be entirely closed and screened by trees or by other means. The Elizabeth Monument in the Elizabeth Garden, Vienna, being

formed as the termination of a narrow alley-way which is an off-
shoot of the park proper, is particularly good in this respect.   In a

Fig. 59.   Back of the Dumas Statue, Paris.

similar manner, when the design is large and is based upon the
complete circle, it should have at least two, and is better with four,

roads approaching upon opposite sides, connected by a large circular sweep bordered with lawns and flowers, and any trees that may be introduced placed in regular and formal positions.

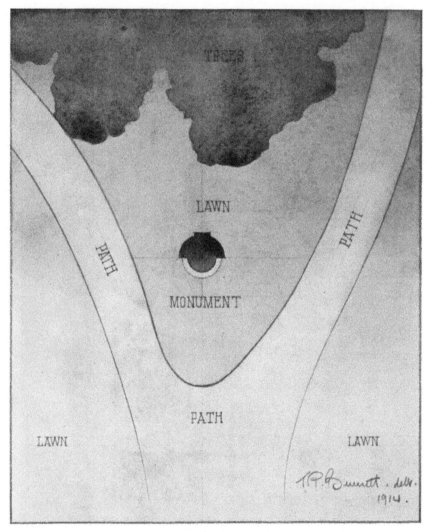

Fig. 60. Plan of the Park Monceau around the Guy de Maupassant Statue, Paris.

Many picturesque situations having special connection with the personage or group can be composed. Ambroise Thomas, in the

Park Monceau, Paris (Fig. 79), seems beautifully in keeping with his surroundings in a dell overhung by trees and within sound of the music of falling water with moss and water-plants climbing over the banks of the small brook, and in spring brilliant little spots of colour appear as one by one the crocus thrusts its modest head above the grass.

The group at the back of the Grand Palais known as Le Rêve du Poéte has similarly harmonious surroundings (Fig. 78). The use of artificial architectural ruins may here be open to criticism. It is false art to produce by design picturesque effects properly belonging to the chance circumstance of time or the accident of occupation.

When an important group is placed in a park it should not be surrounded by rustic seats or features of an allied nature if the sculpture and its accompanying architecture are designed upon formal lines. In such cases all objects in the vicinity of the principal design should partake of a similar character. The seats should be preferably of stone, but may sometimes be of wood and should be designed by the same artist as the monument.

The chief quality of the park should be its pliability, and the whole environment of monuments within its precincts should be in sympathy with the plastic forms.

It is impossible to over-estimate the value of water in monumental work, and only the size necessary and the
The value
and danger of   expense involved should prevent its more frequent
water.
use. The Place Lambermont, previously mentioned,
provides an example where it has been most effectively employed. When a large quantity of water in the form of lake or river is present, the power of its great volume may, unless special allowance be made, kill the whole design. The insistent form of the obelisk upon the embankment lifts it well out of danger from this cause and Cleopatra's Needle, combined with a Sphinx on either side and the Embankment wall (Fig. 92), is one of the most striking and successful monuments in London.

In passing it may be noted that the presence of a great waste of water is, perhaps, the only element which can make the colossal statue a possibility. The Liberty Figure, New York—(Fig. 99) one of the largest—is also one of the most successful.

8—2

CHAPTER VI

THE SMALL MONUMENT

THE increasing tendency to commemorate important personages of contemporary times and to immortalise various great celebrities in their native towns and elsewhere, will probably cause those groups which are here considered under the title of the Small Monument to be even more frequently offered to the sculptor and the architect for solution than they are at present.

When orthodox forms are adopted as a basis of design the limitation of size and cost generally prevent any marked degree of originality in the detail. It must be accepted in these cases almost as a *sine quâ non* that great latitude cannot be allowed for the enrichment of the pedestal, either by the introduction of subsidiary figures, or a large amount of carving, or even the use, on anything approaching a large scale, of bronze accessories.

The limitation of size and cost.

When a single figure upon a pedestal is demanded, it occasionally becomes necessary to study economy in the design of the figure itself. To this the sculptor very rightly has strong objections, and it should be obvious that if he is compelled to do so, something must be wrong with the requirements of the client. Nevertheless, the designer is sometimes faced with the necessity of providing a monument which is out of all proportion to the funds placed at his disposal. The cost of material and labour necessary, the expense of casting, the employment of models, and so forth, leave him totally inadequate remuneration for his work.

But apart from financial difficulties, the bronze figure and the stone pedestal used where there is no possibility of designing special features to connect the two into a complete composition have great artistic disadvantages.

The strong contrast in colour produced between bronze and stone frequently has the effect of disjointing the figure and its base, and the conditions of the problem allow the designer no scope to remedy this serious defect.

The mere placing of a bronze figure upon a pedestal cannot be said to constitute a monument. It is of paramount importance that the two be welded together into one definite whole, so that when complete they exhibit absolute unity of effect. The two elements must be as much part of each other as the roof is part of the building it covers. The projection of foot or drapery over the top of the pedestal is sometimes asserted to be sufficient, but the argument is hardly conclusive. That a mere insignificant shadow a few inches square is capable of combining a bronze figure, over life size, to a pedestal 6' 0" or more in height, is little more than the merest concession to the point, not a fulfilment of its requirements.

Unity.

An obvious way of avoiding the difficulty is to abandon the use of bronze for the figure and to carve it in marble. This frequently produces excellent effect, especially where the background consists of dark foliage or of the black shadow of an opening in a building where the bronze, by virtue of its colour, would partake too much of the tone of the surrounding objects and therefore lack definition. The monotony of a large expanse of white marble can be obviated and a beautiful gradation of tone produced by the use of white or grey granite in conjunction with the marble. In such cases the deeper colour should be below, each successive change becoming lighter until it is finally crowned by the brilliance of the statuary at the top. When the design offers opportunity for so doing, it may be relieved with small bronze ornaments applied to the stone.

The use of marble and other materials.

The lettering of the inscription can be made to fulfil the office of bronze ornament with admirable effect, and only too little consideration is generally given to this point. The inscription, since it must of necessity be used, should be regarded by the sculptor as of inestimable advantage, adding interest to his design, and its careful arrangement will amply repay whatever thought may be expended upon it. A long wordy epistle such as was often used a generation or so ago, is to be avoided. Apart from any other consideration it creates a great mass of rather indefinite forms which are exceedingly difficult

Lettering and inscription.

to handle. One or two groups of letters composed into a band or
a block are comparatively easy to incorporate into the design.   In
addition to this, a brief inscription is almost invariably read. When
the man represented is at all a familiar figure, as is naturally
almost always the case, his name and the date of birth and death
are sufficient, with possibly the addition of one word describing the
work for which he was famous.   When more than this is desired,
it is better to split the lettering into two or more groups ; to place
large letters giving the name upon the principal face where they
form an important part of the composition and at the sides, or
when convenient at the back, a special surface or panel, upon
which the rest of the inscription can be added.   Here it will have
an interest of its own, and be valuable in a position in which the
group cannot be very effective.   The inscription upon the monument outside the National Portrait Gallery, " Henry Irving, Actor,"
conveys an impression that he had complete command of the art
of impersonation, a master of histrionic art—as indeed he was—no
more is needed.   The mention of his honours seems insignificant
and small. What are empty honours beside the fact of attainment?
" Henry Irving, Actor."   There is finality.

In parks or similar places, colour may be added by means of
Colour intro- flowers, lawn or bushes around the base of the group.
duced by
flowers and The introduction of brilliant reds and yellows, greens
verdure.   and blues, obtained by their use, opens up a field
so vast that it should satisfy, if need be, the veriest glutton for
varied effect.   The manner of planting must depend upon the
requirements of each individual case and the exact nature of the
surroundings.

Originality of conception or the realization of a spontaneous
Originality   idea is all-important.   If these can be obtained and
in conception. the group can be made to express with force and conviction something of the personality of the man in addition to
a representation of his features, interest and distinction, which are
such essential factors, will necessarily follow.

The abandonment of the pedestal and figure for universal use,
has also practical points which are worth consideration.

It does not seem reasonable to commemorate all men, irrespective of their field of work or range of influence, by one monotonous
type of monument.   These groups are generally erected shortly
after the decease of the person concerned, and it is then difficult to

judge his relative greatness. Apart from this, some distinction between the form of monument adopted for the local politician and for the great statesman in addition to the probable difference in size, is useful to give recognition of their respective positions.

The marble or the bronze bust, besides having the additional advantage of overcoming the great artistic difficulties connected with the representation of modern dress, especially the dress of men, suggests a nucleus for a small design which could be used upon a great many more occasions than it has been in the past.

The use of the bust in monuments.

Various forms of relief treatment afford immense scope for originality, and, where the circumstances of the case are suitable, give freedom in handling the subject and suggest possibilities of gradation in the expression and thoughts to be conveyed by means of the design. The versatile French mind has displayed very active qualities of invention in this direction, and both France and Belgium possess many examples of the sculptor's art in bas-relief worthy of the closest attention.

The use of bas-relief.

The use of symbolic ornament is another point which has received all too little attention. The association of certain objects with definite acts and the trend naturally given to the thoughts by this association could frequently be used to add immensely to the force of a design. Their range and variety suggest an inviting means of departing from the time-honoured motifs of the bay-leaf and the egg and tongue, and it is rather extraordinary that more excursions have not been made into so fruitful a field. It must only need the example of a strong man to lead the way for their tremendous value to be realised, and for the use of symbolic objects to become a recognised means whereby a monument may be made to appeal to the mind as well as to the eye.

Symbolic ornament.

By the use of the bust, a monument may be designed upon lines of the utmost simplicity and may yet produce a most charming effect. To support the bust, there are three prototype forms which can be made a basis of design—the column, the Hermes pedestal, and the low truncated obelisk. The French have upon occasion employed the console as a fourth.

Treatments involving the use of the bust.

The column possesses the qualities of grace and distinction. It raises the bust well up to or above the eye-line and its small upper surface provides a very satisfactory seating to receive the sculpture. The material used should be marble or stone for both bust and pedestal. Bronze in this position would be out of place except, possibly, for the inscription; generally even that is better cut in the stone. The column may be designed with a capital and abacus; the bust upon a moulded stand resting upon the top. A very good

Fig. 61. Monument to Armand Silvestre, Paris.

example of this treatment will be found in the garden of the Villa Albani, where there is a most effective range of columns in a yew hedge lining one of the walks.

The monument to Armand Silvestre in Paris (Fig. 61) shows a treatment in which the capital is omitted and the bust connected directly to the shaft. Around the base of the column are introduced small female figures, giving lightness and interest to the complete group. Perhaps these figures are somewhat too fanciful for English ideas, but they are certainly most effective and the whole design shows marked individuality as a departure from accepted lines.

When the bust is used in a street or surrounded by severe architectural forms, the pedestal is best kept severe in character, to maintain harmony with the adjacent work. In these cases the use of specially designed steps or high blocks at the base will go far both to give importance to the actual design and will act as a means of connection with the surrounding ground. When the group stands in a roadway, it needs a fairly wide paved space, or it may bear too much resemblance to a lamp-post or a guard-post, and for the same reason should be placed upon proportionately wide and high blocks so that the pedestrian is unable to touch the sculpture.

The Schiller Monument in New York consists of a simple bust placed upon a plainly-moulded block of stone, but it is surrounded by an elaborate combination of irregular stone steps, rustic wood-work and flowers, so that almost total reliance is placed upon the chance growth of nature trained to appear untrained. This, surely, is false art. The artist should produce a complete work, beautiful in itself. If nature adds qualities to his creation which he did not contemplate, all well and good, but definitely to design picturesque effects so that they appear accidental is a position which should be untenable to a man with high ideals.

The introduction of subsidiary figures allows wide scope for suggestion in these designs. It now becomes possible not only to portray the features of the man but to add an ideal element beautified by the imagination and technical skill of the artist. Care must be taken when such figures are used that the importance of the bust is not reduced by the addition. It is quite easy to add accessories so full of interest that the original motive of the design is lost. The figure, therefore, must be definitely related to the bust and the relation must be obtained in such a manner that it directs the sight and the mind to the personality portrayed. This can generally be ensured by the elevation of the sculptured head above the general level so that it becomes the highest feature of the group.

The monument to Guy de Maupassant (Fig. 62) in the Park Monceau, Paris, shows this relation, and the vertical effect of pedestal and bust are well contrasted with the horizontal lines of the figure below. Parts of the architecture, while distinctly French, are particularly pleasing. Special attention may be given to the deep plinth without mouldings, the single step above, and the construction and outline of the seat. It is worthy of note that the 6″ step next to the ground would have been entirely a mistake,

Fig. 62. Monument to Guy de Maupassant, Paris.

and is not employed. The natural appearance of the folds of the lady's skirt is a feature which the English sculptor should not adopt without great consideration; although attractive in some respects, it is undoubtedly Rococo in tendency and leads towards the abandonment of all convention and restraint. The effect of the placing referred to in Chapter V can be clearly realised from the photograph.

The beautiful situation of the Allewaert Monument in The Park at Antwerp (Fig. 63) shows up its interesting qualities to the greatest advantage. The bust is in white marble, the base in red granite, and the children in bronze; the children exhibit the leaning towards naturalistic representation already mentioned, but are nevertheless delightful little beings. The junction of the base

Fig. 63. Monument to Allewaert, Antwerp.

of the head and the books beneath, with the top of the pedestal, does not seem to be quite harmonious ; the square member crowning the base is a little coarse, and the sudden set-back to the marble leaves a feeling of abruptness. The growth from lawn to flower-bed and from flower-bed to pedestal is excellently arranged. The steps of the base with the joint strongly expressed, show a variation upon the orthodox type which seems satisfactory.

The omission of the ordinarily-accepted step in these two examples is much to be praised. Its use in such situations has no practical object, and the connection with the ground can be much better made by the high block of the first, or by the excellent use of flowers shown in the second.

In England, Mr Goscombe John has produced a very pleasing

Fig. 64. Monument to Sir Arthur Sullivan, Embankment Gardens, London.

group, embracing the head and bust in his design for the Memorial to Sir Arthur Sullivan in The Embankment Gardens (Fig. 64). The relation between the head and the pedestal and the outline of the pedestal itself are very well designed. The figure of Grief is not quite so satisfactory, principally because, if the criticism be allowable, it seems a false idea to perpetuate the fact of the man's death rather than the glorious achievements of his life.

Larger compositions involving the use of the bust are occasionally employed. They are subject to much the same rules and
limitations as the smaller groups The pedestal in this case becomes correspondingly increased in size and importance. A group
of two or three figures and a bust cannot be placed as close to the
eye as it is possible to place such groups as have just been considered. Under the circumstances, it will be found that the circular
base is a most valuable form to use ; it can be made to conform to
the lines of the sculpture much more satisfactorily than the square,
without leaving those awkward angles which tax the ingenuity of
the sculptor to the utmost and then, if it is far above the eye, often
cut across the group at an unfortunate angle. With the employment of two or more figures, increasing importance attaches to the
position in which the bust is to be placed.

The commonly accepted form of small monument in England,
The single   consisting of a single figure standing upon a stone
figure.   pedestal, must be familiar to all.

The first question which almost instinctively arises after a study
of many of these examples is, why should the figure always be
used in a standing attitude?

There are one or two examples of seated figures which are so
eminently successful, and have a mass and outline so superior to
the somewhat disconnected effect of the standing figure, that the
rarity of its employment seems quite extraordinary. In addition
to a change of attitude, the monotony of these monuments could
often be relieved by the use of some object connected with the
man's life. This object might at times be quite large in comparison, without detracting from the importance of the principal
figure. In Saint Gaudens' Monument to Abraham Lincoln at
Chicago, the famous President has been represented as if he had
just risen from a chair to address an assembly. So characteristic
an attitude and the presence of the chair, although not occupied,
leaves no doubt as to the intention of the pose and betokens
brilliant thought on the part of the sculptor.

Mouldings upon the pedestal, if at all heavy, or if given much
projection, make sympathetic connection between figure and base
extremely difficult to obtain, and they could in many instances be
dispensed with almost entirely, to the great advantage of the
group. The strength of the shadow immediately under the figure
caused by an overhanging cornice and the insistent nature of many

horizontal lines, do not tend to produce harmony between the sculpture and its base. This may be to some extent overcome by raising the group above the top of the cornice by a high blocking.

A comparison between the two statues placed one on either side of the Nelson column is a rather striking illustration of the value to be gained by the omission of mouldings. The base to the

Fig. 65. Monument to Charles Napier, Trafalgar Square, London.

statue of General Napier (Fig. 65) has a simple battered face finished at the top with a plain off-set; out of this the figure grows in a beautifully easy manner. It is true that the arrangement of the cloak contributes to the harmonious effect, but nevertheless it has not the feeling of disconnection caused by the shadow in the other example, a point which is realised more fully in an actual examination than it is in a photograph. The Sir Henry Havelock group (Fig. 66) is further interesting for comparison because it is not too far removed in point of date and partakes to some extent of the same character. The admirable connection obtained by the suppression of mouldings in the study of many examples has led to the conviction that it is a most desirable end at which to aim.

Fig. 66. Monument to Sir Henry Havelock, Trafalgar Square, London.

This more particularly refers to the single figure used upon a square pedestal. The circular pedestal under a single figure and that of whatever shape used for a large group will generally require mouldings. The value of drapery to a standing figure is very great, and when used around the back, the broad enclosing lines have a restful effect which is very pleasing, besides enclosing the broken shadows which generally occur in the front view, especially

in connection with the legs. The conventional frock-coat, which
causes so much trouble, if insisted upon, should be treated as
enclosing drapery.   If buttoned up, it will give a most unpleasant
effect, necessitating, as it does, the use of a large circular shape in
bronze or marble around the figure, beneath which will protrude

Fig. 67. Monument to Teniers, Antwerp.

two legs. If unbuttoned, the direction of the lines from the pedestal
upwards is not harshly broken and the large planes of light and
shade surrounding the figure can be turned to advantage.

The base of the monument, when in a public square, in a situation already prepared for its reception, should not have steps in the

ordinary sense of the term. The plinth of the Napier Monument
coming directly on the pavement is quite satisfactory. Sometimes,
when the group stands upon grass or where flower-beds are placed
around, it can advantageously be designed with blocks at the base
of quite considerable height, but when upon paths, roadways, or in
similar situations the use of the ordinary step in some form becomes

Fig. 68. Monument to President McKinley, San Francisco.

a necessity. In such circumstances, the circle of paving combined
with a square base is often effective.

The circular paving under the Teniers Monument in Antwerp
(Fig. 67) is extremely valuable in bringing the group into relation
with the road, and the large square block above assists it very
greatly.

The base of the monument to President McKinley in San Francisco (Fig. 68) has an even stronger sweep of circular steps, which form quite an important feature in the design. In this case they are upon a large scale, the top step being 44′ 0″ in diameter, and admirably maintain the feeling given to the commanding figure of the Republic upon the top.

Fig. 69. Monument to Quinten Matsys, Antwerp.

The difficulty experienced in maintaining the same scale and treatment in both the sculpture and architecture is well illustrated in these two groups. The fine richness of the ornament upon the pedestal of the Belgian group makes it an excellent piece of architecture; the simple lines of the panel and the plain lettering of the inscription below show admirable restraint. This richness is carried

into the modelling of the figure, but the sculpture hardly manages
to achieve the richness of the architecture; the scale of the figure
appears slightly too small, and the composition suffers considerably
in consequence. In the McKinley group, on the other hand, the
sculpture has a breadth of treatment and force of design which the
more refined, but less vigorous architecture seems unable to maintain. The steps revert to the scale of the figure, and so go far to
bind the composition together.

The circular pedestal for the single figure has special advantage, as was pointed out for treatments of figures and a bust.
The harmony between sculpture and architecture in the Quinten
Matsys group—a Gothic design (Fig. 69)—is quite obvious, and
the effect of this statue is extremely good. The movement
always present in a circular scheme is well steadied by the square
block at the base and the emphasis given to the angles by the
introduction of four lamps. These lamps are painted black, and
are somewhat too heavy for the rest of the group. The treatment
adopted for the inscription gives a very pleasant introduction of
colour. The pedestal is of grey stone, and the panel containing
the inscription is gilded. Upon this is the lettering—the capitals
in red and the rest of the letters in black.

The square base with splayed angles may next be considered.
This shape has more strength than the circle, which in some cases
is a valuable asset. Oliver Cromwell, at the Houses of Parliament
(Fig. 70), is a very successful example of its use, showing good
proportion between the size of the splay and the breadth of the flat
face. Where the splay lower down develops into a definite feature
with a special crowning member, it becomes of great value to the
design. This example may be used to show the importance of
obtaining good main lines for the composition and of not attempt-
ing to vary them in various portions of the scheme. The high
weathering above the cornice upon which the figure is placed
brings it into good relation with the pedestal. The introduction of
the bronze lion is a particularly clever piece of design; the lion,
besides the great amount of interest which it creates upon its own
account, echoes the figure in such a manner that the violent contrast in colour which is sometimes a cause of disconnection becomes
a virtue. The inter-relation of the two materials goes far to produce
the unity so necessary to a great work.

Good co-relation between the bronze and stone is obtained in

Fig. 70. Monument to Oliver Cromwell, London.

the somewhat unusual design of the monument to Armand Steurs, in Brussels (Fig. 71). The pedestal is composed of masonry, practically devoid of mouldings, relieved by vegetation; the great square blocks of stone, simple in detail and having marked individuality in their arrangement, make the composition quite interesting. The bronze group consists of a man and a goat. The man is modelled in a curious attitude with the head and shoulders brought right forward, and has a face which is so grotesque in appearance as to be almost unpleasant. But while the detail of the bronze is open to criticism, the actual mass is satisfactory, and its colour, reflected by the green vegetation on various parts of the base, obtains unity in the green and white effect which is suggested throughout. The combination of particularly hard forms in the stone with the soft lines of the vegetation is full of interest.

The bold and massive outline of the seated figure can be made to compose well with the architectural lines of the base and contains many other features which are valuable assets to the designer. The chair or seat necessary affords a great amount of scope in its design and a means of legitimately introducing additional interest. It is essential that the chair should be so designed that all possibility of mistaking it for a piece of furniture is avoided. The general lines and the detail should be in complete sympathy with the pedestal and seem only a continuation of the base. For this reason it is often safer to make the chair and the figure in stone, rather than in bronze, although it may not always be advisable to do so. When, however, the material is changed it becomes more essential than ever to obtain a seat which cannot by any possibility be related to the commonplace article of household use. In the author's design for a monument to a great scholar, shown in Fig. 72, an attempt has been made to produce a scheme which would by harmonious treatment of the detail and careful relation of the various parts suggest the polished refinement which would have been in all probability a marked characteristic of the living personality. To this end the mouldings are largely subdued and those used are of simple section and carefully proportioned. The relation of the chair to the base in the side elevation received special attention, so that the chair would appear as a continuation of the architecture beneath, and compose into a good group without the sculpture. The use of bronze was avoided so that this relation would be further established.

Fig. 71. Monument to Armand Steurs, Brussels.

While restraint was felt to be so necessary, any suggestion of coldness was equally undesirable, and to avoid this the top of the base is enriched with carved ornament. This ornament is intended not only to give the necessary richness, but also to reflect the broken shadows of the figure above and to carry the feeling of the sculpture into the architectural lines below, until it is lost in the broad and simple lines of the steps.

The figure and chair are to be carved in white marble and the rest of the group in grey granite, the name to be added in bronze letters of Roman type applied singly to the panel prepared for them. This group was modelled for the author and the figure designed by Mr Alexander Stiles.

The range of treatment possible with a single figure necessarily Two-figure restricts the subject, and anything in the nature of an groups. elaborate conception cannot be represented. As a rule, the monument becomes either a portrait-statue which, as previously pointed out, is by far the more common, or the figure represents the embodiment of a single quality or idea. The figure of the Republic used on the McKinley Monument at San Francisco is a good example of the latter. With the use of two figures, however, there is much greater scope, and many of these limitations are removed. The portrait-statue may be combined with an ideal figure if the combination is effected with care; or the group may portray a specific action connected with its object. Groups of this kind are used in connection with the commemoration of a body of men, or an important incident in history, more frequently than with the memory of an individual. Many of them have been connected with war monuments, a favourite theme being the portrayal of a soldier defending or carrying a wounded comrade. Sometimes one of the two is shown in the act of falling, presumably from the effect of a bullet-wound. Such an attitude is open to very serious criticism; humanity in a state of collapse is never a pleasant sight, and even when idealised and modelled in bronze, cannot be regarded as pleasing. The lines produced by the limp falling figure are not good, and very few of these groups can be considered satisfactory compositions.

This defect is very noticeable in the monument to Frederick de Mérode in the Place de Mérode, Antwerp (Fig. 73), more so perhaps because the design otherwise has many excellent points. The simple architectural lines, well proportioned and in good

relation to the group above, are relieved by a bronze lion in front.
The use of a lion in this position, as pointed out in the Oliver

Fig. 72.   Design for a Monument to a Great Scholar.

Cromwell Monument (Fig. 70), is productive of harmonious relationship between the parts, and the modelling in this instance

makes it most interesting in itself, while the flowers and curb connect the whole group to its surroundings in a very satisfactory manner.

Fig. 73. Monument to Frederick de Mérode, Place de Mérode, Antwerp.

In other forms the two-figure group often offers excellent opportunities for design. Particular mention may be made of those groups depicting one figure guarding or protecting another.

The feeling of enclosure thus obtained and the sympathy of line between the two is an admirable quality and adds immensely to the interest. A beautiful effect is obtained from a group of this type in the Cadets Monument in Brussels (Fig. 74). The drapery of the female figure enclosing the youth seems to concentrate attention upon the lovely modelling of the nude figure; the youth goes forth

Fig. 74. Monument to the Naval Cadets, Brussels.

upon his journey into the great unknown scorning protection, although conscious of the immense mystery of death and feeling some temerity. These two figures grow out of the base with an easy and natural grace, which has every appearance of spontaneous thought. Richness in the sculpture must receive recognition in the base, and here it is found in the group of freely-treated trophies at the front. The colour effect has been most carefully studied—grey

LE ANTICHITÀ
ROMANE
DI GIAMBATISTA PIRANESI
ARCHITETTO VENEZIANO
TOMO QVARTO
CONTENENTE I PONTI ANTICHI
GLI AVANZI DE TEATRI
DE' PORTICI
E DI ALTRI MONVMENTI
DI ROMA

Fig. 75. Portion of a Circular Pedestal—Etching by Piranesi.

granite for the curbs and steps, white granite for the pedestal, and white marble for the group. The sweep of the curbs enclosing the flowers at the sides further spreads the lines, and the colour combination, as previously mentioned, adds value to the final effect.

The circular moulded pedestal can often be most advantageously used under a two-figure group. The increase of size gives the designer scope for obtaining good relation between the figure and the pedestal. When the modelling of the figures is particularly rich, it may be echoed by using sculpture in relief upon the base ; a band running completely around under the cornice is one way in which it may be introduced.

A masterly etching by Piranesi of a broken portion of a shaft showing a treatment of this nature is reproduced in Fig. 75. The relation of shapes and surfaces which he obtains is magnificent, and should be capable of adjustment to suit the requirements of a modern design.

The amount of enrichment permissible has been excellently gauged in the Alfred de Musset (Fig. 76) group in Paris, and here again the absence of moulding brings the sculpture directly into touch with the pedestal, making the two absolutely one unit. The attitude of the figure behind de Musset directs attention towards him, and emphasises his importance. The rounded angle with the addition of a simple leaf ornament is a pleasant variation upon the usual splay ; but the small 6″ step upon the pavement cannot be called satisfactory. Far from helping to connect the group to its situation, it seems to have the opposite effect, and would have been better omitted altogether.

There are a few three-figure groups which should receive con-
Three-figure   sideration in this chapter. It will conduce towards
groups.   good composition in such cases if two of the figures can be placed upon a lower level than the third, the latter being the most important. If it is essential for them all to be upon the same level the due subordination of two may be obtained by showing them seated. If placed below, they may be either seated or standing, according to the exigencies of the design.

A very typical English composition, employing three figures generally in bronze, placed at points corresponding to the angles of a triangle, gives satisfactory results. The two lower ones face outwards and are generally seated. The upper one is elevated upon a form resembling the obelisk and may be either seated or standing. This should not be used where all sides are of equal importance, and is better in situations where the front is the view most generally seen. The Gladstone Monument, Liverpool, illustrates this type (Fig. 77). The monument to the Comte de Kerchore der Denterghem in Ghent displays a peculiar feature in the use of nude and draped figures in conjunction. The centre part

Fig. 76. Monument to Alfred de Musset, Paris.

of the group consists of a pedestal upon which is a seated draped figure. In front are two standing figures placed independently upon the lower part of the base, one, that of a man fully clothed, representing Labour, is looking towards and apparently preparing to follow the second, representing Abundance, which is treated in the nude. The juxtaposition of the two has an extremely bad effect. Great care should be taken in the introduction of allegorical figures that they are sufficiently far removed from the natural to show their relation to the ideal. They should never be allowed to challenge comparison as they do in this instance with such fatal result.

The use of bas-relief in the design of monuments for park settings should form a subject of close study. The gradation which can be obtained opens up possibilities

Bas-relief composition.

Fig. 77. Monument to Gladstone, Liverpool.

in the way of suggestion and emphasis which could not be accomplished by any other treatment. If a poet, for example, is to be commemorated, the relief should show him almost in the round, and in the background should be represented various works of his creation—important books or plays by figures in high relief—thoughts to which he gave expression, or ideas stated which were never crystallised may be suggested by figures in very slight relief.

The spectator would thus be carried over the man's work as his eye fell first on one and then upon another of his crea-

Fig. 78.   Relief—"Le Rêve du Poéte," Paris.

tions. When these relief treatments receive a sylvan setting, giving them the poetry of situation to add to the poetry of art,

Fig. 79. Monument to Ambroise Thomas, Paris.

Fig. 80. Monument to Franz Laure, Ghent.

they have a beauty which possesses unlimited power to charm and captivate.

The group called Le Rêve du Poéte at the back of the Grand Palais in Paris (Fig. 78) has many of these qualities: its nebulous outline suggests the poetic fancy of the man and fits the group for informal surroundings, and the addition of water adds to the interest of the group. The modelling in many places is exquisitely rendered and of itself makes the monument a most artistic piece of work.

Ambroise Thomas in the Park Monceau, Paris (Fig. 79), is another group upon similar lines. The situation here, as previously remarked, is even more inviting. The block of marble upon which the group is carved seems as if it cropped out of the ground by accident and the carving was placed upon it while in its place. The whole rendering suggests the musician, the creator of beautiful and harmonious sounds, delighting in the rustle of the tree and the murmur of the brook, and thus not only are the features of the man portrayed, but something of the quality of his spirit becomes infused into his monument.

Franz Laure in the Place Lamont, Ghent (Fig. 80, see also Fig. 55), has, as its situation demands, a more severe treatment. The bold square outline of the wall gives precision and definition to the boundaries of the group. Upon this wall are placed figures modelled in bronze, representing " Philosophy," " Instruction," " Jurisprudence" and " Philanthropy." Colour is introduced by placing the name of the figures in gilt letters upon salmon-coloured marble and these panels are most effective. Franz Laure, himself, as the most important person, is in the round brought well away from the background. Great interest attaches to the whole both for its own sake and also as an original and creative work.

While praising these treatments in relief it is as well to sound a warning note. They have the Rococo seed sown in their free outlines and ungoverned detail. Having interest, individuality, and personal connection with their subject, they may be used with admirable effect as long as they show restraint and a recognition of the laws of order and convention. When these are abandoned, pure Art goes to the four winds and all the wild excesses of the most debased periods become imminent possibilities.

CHAPTER VII

LARGER MONUMENTS

Most of the compositions mentioned in the previous chapter
Type of composition. are unsuitable for use in large and important groups
unless they undergo radical change ; if, therefore, one
of these is suggested by a committee as the type to be followed, it
may be advisable to attempt to obtain an alteration in their views
before proceeding with a sketch model. The three-figure groups
mentioned at the end of the chapter are perhaps an exception and
are probably capable of considerable expansion. Upon the other
hand, where individual features are used which demand a large size
in order that they may retain ordinarily accepted relation to the
human scale, they must only be employed in such compositions as
will allow them adequate expression.

The most important of these, on account of its frequent occurrence, is the equestrian monument. Little horses are
The eques-trian monu-ment. an abomination ; the horse should never be used under
life size and is even then singularly ineffective, by its
bulk it requires a pedestal of considerable dimensions, and if it has
much action it should stand upon a broad surface; added to this is
the fact that the use of a horse gives wide range and greater power
to the figure, and the pedestal must not therefore negative these
qualities by appearing insignificant. To comply with the various
points enumerated, a monument having considerable dimensions is
a necessity. It is one of those instances in which bulk is of itself
desirable; other groups which must be upon a large scale if they
are to be effective are those involving the use of the column or of
The column. the arch. If the column is small it becomes a mere
toy; rather should it go to the other extreme and
appear to belong to the habitation of giants and not to that of
men.

The arch, likewise, should have command and power, suggesting vast resources and sumptuous magnificence to
The arch. which the glories of victory and the spoils of war
have added their grand tribute. The disagreeable effect produced
even in a building by the low arch and the insignificant opening
must be familiar to all, and if such features are considered so
undesirable in places where utilitarian conditions make it difficult
to obtain anything else, they should be far more strenuously
avoided in monumental work.

In the equestrian monument the first item which should receive
attention is the horse; the design of the whole group,
Equestrian monuments. (a) The horse. not only in detail but in outline and general composition, will depend to a large extent upon the treat-
ment adopted. The action is capable of great variation, from a
simple standing pose to a position of the utmost violence, and
it should be governed by two factors: firstly, by the man who
is to be commemorated—this is generally settled beforehand—and
secondly by the type of pedestal to be used, which is generally left
to the decision of the designer.

Every man by virtue of his office represents certain qualities
irrespective of his personal character. Thus the king has power
over men and by his kingship commands submission and obedience
from his subjects. When he is represented in a monument riding
a horse, that horse should be under complete and easy control,
symbolic of his power, yet the animal must not be a tame and
spiritless beast but a thoroughbred, full of restless life and energy
although not daring to assert these qualities under the hand of his
royal master. It should be richly caparisoned and the decorative
qualities of flowing mane and tail used to the greatest advantage.
The body should show grace in build and beauty in pose; the
delicate curve of the neck when the head is bent may lend immense
value to the effect of the whole group. The legs may all be
planted upon the ground as if the king paused and calmly looked
down from his pedestal viewing his subjects and receiving honour-
able acknowledgment from them as they pass by; or one leg may
be raised, not with any suggestion of progression, but in a manner
characteristic of the thoroughbred chafing under restraint, a display
of impatience which all his training has not enabled him to overcome. This will sometimes be useful to introduce variety without
disturbing the calm grandeur of the general effect.

The general, as becomes his warlike calling, has need of a more vigorous horse, displaying energy and strength. The beautiful thoroughbred of the king is quite out of keeping under such a man. A heavier horse should be aimed at here. Whereas the king commands by virtue of his birthright, the general commands by force; he may have a horse held in check by a tight rein and

Fig. 81.   Monument to Joan of Arc, Chinon.

showing some desire to be rid even of this—a suggestion of super-abundant and tireless energy, which is indispensable to a leader of men. It has been the custom recently to make all horses lighter in build, irrespective of the rider, but while upon some occasions this is most praiseworthy it should be done with discrimination. The *bourgeois* leader, such as Garibaldi, may in his monument have a more *bourgeois* type of horse. A good heavy-built substantial animal, such as he would have ridden in his early days, suggests his personality far better than the light riding steed which was perchance his last favourite. The light horse is suited to the prince, beloved for his peaceful deeds in the promotion of intercourse between nations, the development of industries or the governing of dependencies, but it may be changed for an animal of

Fig. 82.   The Colleoni, Venice.

exactly opposite type when he has been a hot-headed, fiery and enthusiastic leader in some hard-fought campaign. An energetic youth, such as the latter, loves an animal full of fight and fire, which it requires all his skill to manage.

Such a fiery animal is suitable also to the fanatic idealist whose fervour and conviction have turned hopeless situations into glorious victory. Joan of Arc (Fig. 81) was such a one; in her case, however, two quite different types have been employed according to the idea intended to be uppermost—her leadership in battle or her deep religious faith in the mission she was called upon to perform. With the utmost action, however, the horse should never lack balance or definite lines of composition. Wild abandoned attitudes or unmanageable animals alike violate the canons of good taste and should not be employed.

Broadly speaking, there are two types of pedestal suitable for
(*b*) The pedestal.   an equestrian statue: the high block, having a com-

Fig. 83.   Monument to Godefroid de Bouillon, Brussels.

paratively small base, of which Verocchio's statue to Bartolomeo Colleoni, Venice (Fig. 82), is such a fine example, and that designed upon broad and massive lines like the Godefroid de Bouillon group in Brussels (Fig. 83).

The high pedestal, although it does in itself almost invariably give good results, should not be employed with every type of horse and rider; when the horse is portrayed in violent action there is a tendency for its situation high above the ground to seem somewhat precarious, a suggestion which is forced upon the mind in spite of its inanimate nature, and the horse should in these cases be broad and low. The high pedestal should be reserved for instances in which a quiet composition is used for the sculpture.

When the monument is made part of a large lay-out it should harmonise with the general scheme and the feeling of its surround-

Fig. 84. Monument to George IV, Trafalgar Square, London.

ings. Horse and figure should be modified in accordance with their position, irrespective of the person portrayed.

Besides the high pedestals of Verocchio's group of the Colleoni and Donatello's Gattamelata, which are so well known as to be beyond criticism, there are many other examples, notably some English ones by Chantrey, who used it in a particularly unadorned manner which sometimes seems to suffer from coldness. Its very

simplicity, however, shows how satisfactory it is as a base. Wellington, outside the Royal Exchange, Sir Thomas Munro at Madras,
and the base to the statue of George IV in Trafalgar Square (Fig.
84), are three examples. The latter shows excellent relation to
the adjacent architecture and must be regarded as a most satisfactory piece of decoration; the horse is somewhat tame in design—

Fig. 85. Monument to Kaiser William I, Elberfeld.

a feeling to which the lack of trappings contributes. The whole
group would have gained immensely had it received a richer treatment. Apart from this, it has a number of good points.

On account of the bulk of an equestrian figure it is a great
(c) The base advantage if some strong form low down in the
of the pedestal. pedestal can be obtained to counterbalance its weight.
This may be a figure, a moulded base, steps, or other features.

The admirable service rendered by the balustrade of the Hôtel
de Ville to the Étienne Marcel group in Paris (Fig. 48) has
been considered previously.   If the monument is isolated and the
high pedestal employed, this quality of balance may be obtained
by using wide, spreading steps or by a sweeping line in the base
itself; this sweeping line is most effective when it is stopped by
some strong feature, such as a high square plinth block, to prevent
the swing running away and giving a loose composition.   The
monument to the Kaiser William at Elberfeld (Fig. 85) is an
admirable example of this treatment.   The curve here starts well
up from the bottom and the square blocking courses below give
precision and strength at their junction with the ground.   The
lines of the modelling of the horse suggest a continuation of the
lines of the architecture and in this way produce harmony and
cohesion between the two parts.

A carpet flower border planted on a bank below the actual base
adds to the interest of the design, providing a splash of colour
which is echoed by the green of the bronze above.

High pedestals standing upon plain blocking courses are particularly suitable to street sites where the base is seen only through
a kaleidoscope of traffic.   They may well be kept quite simple and
combined with paving and guard posts to give effect; the height
to which the group is raised brings it well into the sight of the
pedestrian upon the footpath.

It will be noticed in the Elberfeld monument that a figure is
introduced at the foot of the pedestal and helps the
composition immensely, both by its colour value and
also by the *naïveté* of idea in the placing of a child's
form close to the warlike horse and the imposing emperor.

(*d*) The en-
richment of
the pedestal.

A standing figure has sometimes been attempted in a similar
position, but it requires most careful handling to make it a success.
There is a tendency for the figure to become detached from the
general composition, but this may be overcome when the lines
of the base curve outwards as they do in Fig. 85 ; if the action
of the figure suggests connection with equestrian group; or by
placing the figure close against the architecture and enclosing it
with a frame when the base is designed upon more severe lines.

The side elevation is frequently of importance and the equestrian
group lends itself well to a side effect ; when approach roads or
other obvious reasons justify its use, the bronze group or bronze

figure can be placed upon the side. In such cases, the upper part
of the pedestal should have vertical sides and the spread of the
base necessary to balance the design should be obtained by these

Fig. 86. Monument to Giuseppe Garibaldi, Rome.

bronzes, and the pedestals and steps used for their reception and
support.

If groups are used upon the sides only, there is a tendency for
the insistence given to the shorter axis to be too great and to com-

pete with the opposite lines of the pedestal and horse. This is not always the case and two groups can be made completely satisfactory. When, however, four groups are used, as in the Garibaldi Statue, Rome (Fig. 86), there is no danger of this defect. This particular monument composes very well and is full of interest ; the figure at the top, both by its fine outline and by virtue of its commanding position, dominates the composition and is able to maintain the supremacy of interest which its importance demands, the other groups being duly subordinated. It is well to bear in mind the different purposes served by the several parts of the composition and to prevent the subsidiary groups around the base gaining undue interest and competing with the central figure.

When the equestrian figure used is designed upon broad strong lines, its combination with a low and massive base generally gives a better result than if the high pedestal is employed. The bold and sumptuous outline of the group to Godefroid de Bouillon in Brussels (Fig. 83) would destroy a high base designed with small mouldings and fine detail, but the vigorous architecture of the block upon which it stands harmonises excellently with the feeling produced by the sculpture and yet has sufficient plain surface to give the necessary contrast.

In this case, the enclosing railing which is often so destructive of atmosphere, is placed sufficiently far away and is low enough in proportion to enter into the composition, adding considerably to the effect, and it is greatly helped by the granite posts which mark its division into bays.

The modern love of free treatment leads to the introduction of bas-relief in many forms. An Italian version is shown in the monument to Prince Amodeus of Savoy (Fig. 87), which possesses many good qualities and some bad ones. It has originality, vitality, vigour and effect, besides the interest which attaches to the detail of the modelling, and full advantage has been taken of the splendid amount of scope which such a scheme allows. On the other hand, the broken outlines and feeling of motion produced by many figures portrayed in a variety of poses are somewhat distracting and are not altogether sound design, having too much suggestion of broken Rococo forms. If such a criticism is attached to this example, it is doubly necessary for the Joan of Arc at Chinon (Fig. 81). It seems a pity that such violent sculpture should have been allied to a singularly refined and scholarly treatment in

the base.   The whole design of this, even to the smallest details,
shows careful consideration.   The rhythm and variety created by

Fig. 87.   Monument to Prince Amodeus of Savoy, Turin.

the short stumpy granite posts and chain, placed only at the sides,
is only one of many good points.

The architectural portion of a large monumental work is not
merely a pedestal upon which sculpture appropriating almost all

the interest and attention is to be placed. It becomes a vital factor

Figure compositions. in the composition and it is even more necessary than before to obtain refinement, balance, symmetry and intrinsic value in the various shapes and masses. The application of enrichment, whether in the form of ornament or of the figure, means emphasis to certain parts, and the success of the whole will depend as much upon the position in which this enrichment is placed as it will upon the excellence of its detail. The sculptor frequently spends so much of the time which he devotes to study to the perfection of detail, the attainment of ability to translate the subtle beauty of the human figure into stone or marble, that his outlook tends to become confined to the consideration of the lines of the figure rather than given to the effect of the whole monument. The fact is frequently overlooked that the vast majority of spectators only see the group from a distance, when the distribution of the masses and the interrelation of the parts is all-important and the detail of the modelling cannot be appreciated. The very last thing the author wishes to do is to belittle excellence of technique or the value of a poetic rendering of plastic forms, and he certainly would not suggest a monument designed for the benefit of the casual observer, but it is vitally necessary to obtain a good general scheme before considering the detail at all. If this is not done the monument will never be of sufficient interest to the observer to attract the close attention which the rendering of its detail may deserve.

The circular pedestal as a base for the central group of a large monument has been adopted upon some occasions with most satisfactory results, and when it is beneath a single standing figure hardly any better form could be found. The fine sweep of the circular lines of the cornice, and possibly also of a moulded blocking, connect sculpture above and architecture beneath with an ease and simplicity which the square form cannot rival. If symbolic seated figures used in conjunction are placed against the lower part of the pedestal, they will help towards the creation of a most harmonious base. Three or four figures are better than two, and the circular base should be designed in such a manner that it recognises their position. A panel sunk into the face of the pedestal, making a frame around the sculpture, or sometimes a raised vertical band acting as a background, will emphasise the

Fig. 88. Monument de la République, Paris.

relationship between the architecture and the sculpture to the great advantage of both.

It is even more essential in a large scheme than it is in a small one that none of the sculpture should be down upon the eye-line. The sculpture, to obtain value, must by its position as well as in conception and treatment, be removed from the material human being. The distance may be obtained either by the design of the lay-out; by height; or by the two used in conjunction. Monumental sculpture which can be touched is invariably incongruous and unsatisfactory.

The Monument de la République, Paris (Fig. 88), embraces in a magnificent group of heroic scale many of the points enumerated. Particularly fine in outline and mass is the upper part of the pedestal, while the crowning figure, and the fine band of bronze bas-relief panels are equally worthy of praise. The distribution of the bronze in this example is very well managed and most characteristic. The trophy under the cornice illustrates a very favourite French method of enrichment.

Of a somewhat different type is the Bismarck Monument in Berlin (Fig. 89), and this, in its own way, has many good features. The hardness and strength given to both the figure of Bismarck and to the circular pedestal are particularly appropriate in the expression of so dominating a personality, and serve to give individual expression to the group. Although the subsidiary figures are completely detached from the central shaft, they maintain a unity of effect which is very marked. This is secured principally by the general similarity of feeling displayed by the various parts.

Sympathetic understanding between sculptor and architect where they are working in co-operation is one of the most necessary as it is sometimes one of the most difficult points to achieve. This example shows the enormous gain to the monument when it is obtained.

Although no one would attempt to confine the use of the square pedestal to the seated figure, yet it cannot be denied that the lines of the chair and the drapery are more in sympathy with a rectangular form than is the general outline of the standing figure.

In a large composition where either three or four subsidiary figures are employed they are most effective when combined with a circular pedestal. One or two figures should be used with a design

based upon the square. One subsidiary figure finds its most
effective if not its only situation in the front, on the principal axis

Fig. 89.   Monument to Bismarck, Berlin.

of the monument. Here it echoes the bronze above, attracting
attention by its colour and its interest, but not, unless unduly

insistent, competing with the principal group which has the emphasis of position and of its silhouette against the sky.

The three-figure composition mentioned in the previous chapter, is capable of use upon a larger scale, but if a similar grouping is retained and the architecture made relatively more important, the result is usually more satisfactory than if the whole design is merely increased in size. The square form of the upper part may be repeated below, partaking somewhat of the nature of a platform provided that it does not become disconnected. If the whole group is raised upon a grass bank or surrounded by flower-beds, or a box hedge, it will contribute to the unification of the mass by the isolation thus obtained.

A particularly pleasing group based upon a square design is the Arany Monument in Budapest (Fig. 90). The architectural forms and the detail are alike good, having refined, well-proportioned mouldings, and sufficient enrichment to prevent the divorce of the plain masonry from the rich plastic forms. The bronze of the near figure has a most interesting composition, and receives great value from the expressive circle of the shield at its side. The broad and important base and the planted border are both found in this example.

The square base, when figures are desired upon its diagonals should always have at least a slight splay. A sharp angle running up behind the centre of a figure is most unsatisfactory, besides necessitating a wide space between the masses of the central block and the mass of the sculpture. It is better if by some means this splay can be made to suggest a background without losing the squareness of the pedestal. An approximation to an octagon is not always desirable. When there is any tendency towards this, it will probably be better to abandon the square and adopt the pure circle.

The obelisk treatment for a figure composition could hardly have a better advocate than the Gambetta Monument in Paris (Fig. 91). It is not in this instance crowned by the principal group, but forms the screen against which it is placed. The sculpture thus becomes the focal point of the whole composition, while the triangulation of subsidiary features, which always makes a satisfactory group, is obtained by the distribution of the other figures. The silhouette of this group is particularly successful, crowned as it is with a contrast of line between the wings of the griffin and the vertical figure on the top and gradually spreading

Fig. 90. Monument to Arany, Budapest.

Fig. 91. Monument to Gambetta, Paris.

until its lower boundaries are marked by the precision of the blocks under the seated figures at the bottom.

The colour of the bronze groups reflected in applied ornament, helps towards the proper relation of the parts, and the stone shield motif, striking a high note above the principal part of the composition, is a particularly praiseworthy piece of design.

While the architectural detail of monuments is often so valuable and interesting in combination with sculpture, the purely architectural monument is as a rule not at all satisfactory. Architecture robbed of utilitarian purpose loses all reason for existence. Beauty of line and harmonious massing, excellent features when a specific purpose calls them into life, are apt to seem futile when used solely for their own sake. When the scheme becomes extremely large and is an important structure in itself, the case is very different although even here the final result is as a rule more satisfying when symbolic sculpture or a large portrait figure is an element in the composition.

All monuments, from the greatest to the least, should have the interest and decorative value of sculpture combined with the setting and character given by architectural forms. Used alone, either loses considerably from the qualities which the other would have supplied.

Perhaps the dust of Egypt can never be shaken from the strongly individualistic form of the obelisk and it may be doomed to appear a foreign element by whatsoever nation adopted.

The obelisk.

Yet as a basis of design it possesses all the distinction of finality coupled with the vitality of a vertical feature. It is true that its insistent nature sometimes makes it difficult to handle, but the existence of one or two excellent monuments in which the obelisk is the principal feature, should be sufficient encouragement for a designer of originality and talent to make further attempts in this direction.

Colossal size is of itself no recommendation. It obtains effect merely by bulk and not by artistic idea or individual treatment. Monuments such as that at Bunker Hill, Boston, U.S.A., although they may have value of a kind, should not be employed by an artistic people. Anyone can create effect by size if he have money to spend, and labour to command.

When, however, an obelisk of reasonable size is incorporated with other features the case is different. It is essential for good design that contrast should be obtained, and to contrast with the vertical obelisk a horizontal form or a suggestion of a horizontal form is best. The most obvious is the colonnaded screen. Scale and space are necessary when such a scheme is adopted, but the final effect will repay the outlay. The upper part of the obelisk should rise above the screen and the columns should be carried around behind. When for any reason the fully developed colonnade cannot be employed, it may be suggested by the use of short square shafts with openings between, crowning a blank wall. In this case the top of the base of the obelisk should generally be as high as the wall and the whole length of the shaft be carried above, but much depends upon individual treatment.

In the case of "Cleopatra's Needle" on the Embankment (Fig. 92), London, the employment of a sphinx upon either side produces a horizontal suggestion, which is very effective, and the fine detail of the bronze coupled with an excellent attachment of shaft and base leave little to be desired.

The enormous decorative value of this monument can be well appreciated if it is viewed from the top of any of the adjacent buildings where more account can be taken of the sweep of the balustrade of the Embankment. The fine shaft rising through the mist of the river on a November day, with a red sun throwing strange lights through the holes of dense clouds, is a most impressive sight and one to fire the imagination of almost any man possessing an artistic personality.

Another satisfactory composition can be obtained by the use of a figure, preferably in bronze, at the foot of the base block. This treatment requires a broad surface of paving or steps shaped for the two component parts of the design, so that they may not appear disconnected, and also to prevent an abrupt junction with the ground.

It has become fashionable to condemn the column as a motive for monumental design, due partly to the fact that one or two attempts to use it upon a large scale have resulted in almost complete failure. It might have been more reasonable, before passing such scathing judgment to have endeavoured to discover whether the motive or the individual designer were at fault. Upon traditional grounds it must always have a certain claim upon the imagination. The greatest victories of the parent race of Rome find remembrance to this day in the

The column.
(a) General design.

names of emperors attached to monumental columns.   It is even
doubtful if Trajan's column is not more notorious than any other
work he ever executed, and the contemporary occurrence of the

Fig. 92. "Cleopatra's Needle," London.

classic revival in architecture and the victories of Wellington and
Nelson have invested it with a new meaning in English eyes.
Further, its appeal is not confined to the Briton, but many French
and also many German examples are to be found.

Since the column at times of great national prosperity has been honoured by such wide and general employment, it should receive sympathetic consideration for contemporary work.

One of the most fruitful causes of failure is that the ordinary utilitarian shaft is taken, and without any important change in treatment or manner of use is transformed into a monument. Any element of a building designed and perfected for a specific purpose suddenly shorn of all surroundings and all the objects which called it into existence would look useless and absurd, and the column, one of the most structural features, cannot be expected to prove an exception.

As the principal part of a monument, it must, like every other portion of a design, conform to new environment and circumstance. It is now a decorative and not a utilitarian object. It has only to support a single sculptured figure and not the weight of lintel, frieze and cornice. It grows from the ground alone, having all the importance of isolation and is not merely one unit in a long range of similar features. Every one of these alterations in purpose requires a corresponding change in design. Because it is decorative (b) The before it is useful it should be much enriched either shaft. with flutes, the combination of flutes and reeds, the French husk or the spear ornament. Horizontal bands may be placed around the shaft at various points. The lower portion may have lictor's rods or it may receive variety and interest by a treatment of figures in bas-relief and there is always the spiral band of relief hallowed by the names of Trajan and Napoleon.

The capital is no longer a cushion acting as a buffer to great (c) The superimposed weight, therefore its projection should capital. be reduced. It may be increased in richness especially if of the Doric order and the abacus need not necessarily be square. A figure, large rather than small in proportion, will form a satisfactory terminal, provided it is carefully connected to the top of the cap, and does not sink below the sight-line from an ordinary point of view.

The lower part provides the greatest scope for originality. No (d) The greater mistake could be made than to place it upon base. the orthodox square-moulded pedestal, displaying pedantic correctness and paucity of imagination.

The base should be seized upon by the artist to be welded into fine shapes and rich forms growing from the ground by steps and blockings branching into interest and play of light and shade until the shaft rises from the centre in such a way that it is impossible to say where a base ends and column begins.

The monumental column, by reason of its isolation, is in danger (e) Types of losing apparent bulk. The Doric order, more and examples. massive in proportion, is, therefore, better than the

Fig. 93. The Victory Monument, Berlin.

Corinthian, but a modified Corinthian cap on a shaft approaching Doric proportion is an experimental possibility, especially if used in conjunction with a Doric colonnade at the base. The Victory Monument in Berlin (Fig. 93) is designed upon these lines. The scale is enormous but good proportion retains balance in the composition and it does not become oppressive. The mass of the main shaft showing through the colonnade gives substance and structure to the design, while to the lower part the bold square block enriched with bas-relief panels lends an air of solidity.

The crowning figure seems inclined to be coarse and the detail of the capital is rather weak and unsatisfactory.

The Duke of York's Column in London (Fig. 94), a more or less commonplace design, achieves a great deal of distinction by

Fig. 94. The Duke of York's Column, London.

virtue of its good proportion and the benefit of a carefully planned and effective setting.

When viewed from the Green Park, high up on the sky-line with great broad masses of steps in front, it is quite an imposing monument, especially towards evening upon a clear day, when practically the whole height is in strong silhouette against the deep blue of a late sky.

The Wellington Column, Liverpool (Fig. 95), suffers from its surroundings nearly as much as the previous example gains. The buildings at the back and sides cut across at various angles and give no value at all.

St George's Hall stretching away in front is so powerful a piece of architectural design that any isolated feature tends to

Fig. 95. The Wellington Column, Liverpool.

become insignificant. In spite of these disadvantages it has some pleasing qualities. A simple base enriched with a bas-relief panel on each face seems to accord with the severe surroundings and the three plain blocks which raise it above the paving have a directness and precision which are extremely valuable qualities.

The Column de Congrès in Brussels (Fig. 96) is in great contrast with the plainness of the Wellington Column, Liverpool.

The shaft is treated in a very rich manner and the base well spread, the principal defect being that the column itself is sunk below the ordinary street level, which detracts considerably from its apparent height and importance, although the paved space around the base gives it connection to the ground. The figure in this instance seems if anything a little high above the abacus.

Fig. 96. The Column de Congrès, Brussels.

The monumental arch, like the Victory Column, must be designed in a suitable manner for the object which it is called upon to serve. A suggestion of the common doorway of every-day use, like the transference of the utilitarian shaft to a monumental setting, is foredoomed to failure.

The trium-
phal arch.

When the arch is an approach to a park, to an avenue, or to a drive, it has an apparent purpose which is of inestimable advantage,

and should be considered indispensable. The derelict appearance
of the Marble Arch since the alteration of the roadway seems likely
to remain one of London's eye-sores for many years to come.

Fig. 97. The Wellington Arch, Constitution Hill, London.

The use of an arch as an approach, however, sometimes suggests
the adoption of the triple composition of the arches of Constantine
and Septimus Severus. These are much more difficult to design

than the single opening type and are rarely so successful. In fact, there are practically no modern examples worthy of mention. Of the single arch the one at the top of Constitution Hill, London (Fig. 97), may now be regarded as worthy of high rank.

The bald unconvincing sky-line, unsatisfactory in any structure, is doubly so in a decorative group and the immense gain which has resulted from the addition of Captain Adrian Jones' quadriga

Fig. 98. The Arc de Triomphe, Paris.

is an object lesson more forcible than any statement of principle or assertion of fact could ever hope to be.

But while this example obtains effect by the fine sculpture with which it is crowned, the Arc de Triomphe in Paris (Fig. 98) has achieved perhaps even greater splendour in other directions. The proportion of the opening, which is rather over $1\frac{1}{2}$ squares high, and also the proportion of the whole mass, are particularly good, and the magnificent entablature and attic show the accomplished and vigorous treatment of the French in one of their finest phases. The situation of this monument, high above the centre of the city, with a formal lay-out entered by twelve roads, contributes very largely towards making it one of the finest monuments in Europe.

The isolated arch needs a depth of reveal which would be quite

Fig. 99.   The Liberty Statue, New York Harbour.

unnecessary in an ordinary design where it forms part of a building, and this should always be given. Even an excessive thickness will be in all probability an advantage rather than a fault. Looseness in the composition is another danger which must be avoided; the wide spreading arch is always unsatisfactory as is also spreading sculpture upon the top. The quadriga when used should be closely knit, as is the London example; neither horses nor any attendants should have much space between, or they will, by their sky-line placing, be liable to become badly disconnected.

The colossal figure has fortunately been rarely used in recent times. Its employment as a rule is out of place, and there are few situations in which it is really satisfactory.

The colossal figure.

If in any situation in close proximity to buildings, the scale of one or the other is killed. The figure generally appears coarse or the architecture paltry and weak. When the Greeks designed colossal figures for their temples, they had a reason in making a representation of a god so much larger than a man, but the modern man cannot offer such an excuse as justification.

The colossal figure in Munich never seems to be satisfactory although the detail is inoffensive enough, and the proportions of the figure are carefully kept.

The Statue of Liberty in New York Harbour (Fig. 99), however, is not nearly so much open to criticism, and it may be the proximity of the vast expanse of water which here makes the treatment possible. Cost will probably limit the use of these gigantic forms to positions in which there is a special reason for their employment.

When a large scheme is desired, scale and mass should be produced by architecture and the sculpture reduced to reasonable size employed in what is its proper sphere as enrichment. Large schemes involving decorative architectural sculpture have a fascination and value which far exceeds the impression created by magnified sculptured forms used alone.

CHAPTER VIII

LARGE MONUMENTAL LAY-OUTS

IN great monumental lay-outs the figure of the actual man who

Importance of the general conception. is the subject of commemoration becomes of minor —sometimes almost of infinitesimal—importance, and no attempt should be made to design sculpture upon a scale which would enable it to compete with great architectural conceptions or dominate a wide area of formal surroundings. The whole energy and inventive genius of the artist should be concentrated upon the production of a scheme which would give expression, not to the features, but to the personality of the man. In many cases the aim might be even higher than this and the monument made to symbolise national life during the period represented by his life.

Lay-outs such as those considered here are often used to

National symbolism. commemorate a departed monarch—the representative figure-head of a nation. The monument in such a case should include not only a portrait statue of the king, but also the outstanding features and developments of the nation during his reign—the absorption of colonies, the development of great industries, the value of the arts, or the glory of a successful campaign.

Great monumental schemes are a splendid financial investment if they remind the populace of the distinction gained in various ways by great men in the past, inspiring the people to emulate their example and continue on the path of progress. No force is so potent as that of ambition firing the sons with a desire to become more brilliant than their fathers—to rise to even greater heights than those attained by the achievement of their predecessors. When the great men are forgotten, when the youth of the present imagines in his conceit that he is far better than any who have gone before or than any who can come after, the canker of decay has begun, and he is a superman indeed who can thereafter stop its progress.

The idea of the collection of great names and personalities around a sovereign seems to open a magnificent field to the imagination. Perchance it is possible to go further and to introduce a bust or a statue of the most outstanding men into the scheme. If to the interest of the architecture of a colonnade were added at intervals of every few bays a sculptured figure of a great painter, musician or statesman, the completed composition would be pulsating with the life of the period it was designed to represent.

With work upon the scale here considered the possibilities are so vast and the examples comparatively so few that they cannot be considered under definite headings, as were those of former chapters. Each scheme has been developed upon the lines which have seemed most natural to the particular circumstances of the case, or are the individual expression of the artist employed.

The architecture must, however, be predominant in all cases, and the sculpture only used to add enrichment by its beauty and poetic expression. Some features are particularly suitable to the purpose in hand. Of these the colonnade is one of the most valuable, but mention may also be made of the terrace, the great external stairway, the tower, and the canopy; interest can also be gained by the use of the single figure, the horse, the lion, or the quadriga—in bronze, in gilt, or in marble.

Predomination of the architecture.

One essential point should never be overlooked, and that is, the necessity of obtaining an adequate and suitable setting so that the surroundings will give expression to the actual design.

The setting.

So long as it fulfils its office a commercial building brought into existence for a particular purpose can be condoned even if it seems somewhat confined in position or hampered by its surroundings; but a monument cramped and uncomfortable has no excuse whatever, and if it cannot be carried to a logical conclusion should never be begun. Trees, lawn, flower-beds, pathways and carriage-drives are part of its body and a good deal of its spirit—without them it becomes little more than a very beautiful corpse.

What greater anomaly could be imagined than a fine processional road such as exists from Buckingham Palace to Trafalgar Square, with a great triumphal archway at its termination, delivering the monarch upon the shores and hoarding which respectively support and screen the raw end of a broken building? Such a thing should be intolerable to any nation, and yet quibbles drag on interminably as to whether half a house can be pulled down or whether the nation can afford to buy the freeholder and eject him altogether.

In Germany, in recent years, some excellent monuments have been erected in various parts of the country, and these groups are all most interesting. They possess originality and distinction which claim attention whether their detail can always be given unqualified praise or not.

The group situated at the junction of the Rhine and the

The Kaiser Monument at The German Corner.

Moselle, at a spot known as "The German Corner" (Fig. 100), is very typical of this work. It stands upon, perhaps, one of the finest sites that could possibly be obtained. The waters of the two rivers flow past, washing each side of the steps, which are placed at the base, and above these the monument itself is built of granite blocks, with a rock-face rising in great bold masses piled one above the other and crowned by a bronze equestrian statue of Kaiser Wilhelm I, attended by a figure of Victory, looking out over the bend of the river. The roughness of the masonry does not, however, become coarse. It achieves richness and breadth while still retaining refinement in detail. The short, stumpy, circular-headed posts which occur on each side of the steps near the water's edge have masterly strength in their bold and simple form, and this strength of feeling is carried on by the piers of the balustrade which break the regular circle of its outline as a sequence of expressive features. The commanding bronze group which crowns the whole is in beautiful harmony with the rest, and worthy of its position in the general composition.

The massive qualities of the monument at The German Corner

The Kaiser Monument, Porta, West-phalia, Germany.

are obtained again in the Kaiser Monument, Porta, Westphalia (Fig. 101). Its tower-like form rises upon the sky-line, so that the rugged outline and fine proportion receive all the emphasis they can possibly obtain. The semi-Gothic character peculiar to some

Fig. 100. The Kaiser Monument at the German Corner, Coblenz.

Fig. 101.   The Kaiser Monument, Porta, Westphalia.

German work is here felt; the work is, perhaps, not quite so pure as that of the previous example, yet it has a harmony with its wild surroundings which is very pleasing. Again the effect of the powerful sweep of the circle is seen, giving value to the base, and it is largely assisted by the stair winding up around the sides, which serves also as a connection between the giant size of the main portion and the scale of the ordinary human being.

The problem of the proper relation of the principal figure to an architectural canopy is often most difficult to solve, but is here accomplished in a particularly satisfactory manner, and a piece of brilliant design is seen in the arrangement of the lettering of the panel in front. Two vigorous shields, carved with representations of the German eagle, act as forceful stops at each end, and are connected by letters of a square nature which compose into a band of ornament between. The smaller part of the inscription breaks the plain surface of the rest of the panel without interfering with the general lines of its composition.

The William I Monument on the Kyffhauser (Fig. 102), on

The Kaiser Monument on the Kyffhauser, Thuringia.

somewhat similar lines, is, perhaps, not quite as effective. Rising from a hillside, a fairly large lay-out of steps and terraces must be passed before the final monument is reached, and these, coupled with the advantage of the natural fall of the ground, give it a bold and majestic outline by throwing it against the sky. The bronze figure seems well placed in the centre of a field of architecture, like a sparkling gem set in a field of gold. The steps compose into a most decorative feature; but a danger which their use upon a large scale entails is the possibility of seriously interfering with the principal part of the group when viewed from some of the most important points of view.

The Kaiser Monument in Berlin (Fig. 103) is a monument

The Kaiser Monument, Berlin.

of parts. The conception of the scheme, with its great colonnade terminating in two fine pavilions and enclosing a central pedestal, supporting the bronze figure of the Kaiser, must be accorded the highest praise, but when the various parts come to be considered in detail they are found to be overloaded with ornament. Sculpture requires time, labour, thought, ingenuity and great skill for its production, and it should never, under any circumstances, be applied with so lavish a hand as to suggest that these qualities are negligible.

Fig. 102. The Kaiser Monument on the Kyffhauser, Thuringia.

Fig. 103.   The Kaiser Monument, Berlin.

Every portion of the pedestal, in this instance, is enriched : standing winged figures are placed close against the base, seated figures upon the steps, and lions guarding flags which project in all directions are placed upon salient blocks detached from the central mass. Much of this detail is loosely applied and becomes the weak spot in an otherwise excellent composition. The quadrigas to north and south Germany upon the two pavilions have a most commanding effect, and the fine figure, upright and bold, is given immense value by the use in each case of the standard. The architecture below displays refinement and some originality, but the decorative sculpture suffers from the same faults as that in the centre. Sufficient depth is gained in the return to give solidity and a suggestion of enclosure without any feeling of cramping.

The situation is not altogether satisfactory; rising upon one side from the river, and facing the high front of the palace, it emphasises the difficulties which are invariably encountered when an attempt is made to place a large monumental group in the heart of a crowded city.

The most recent and the most striking monumental work of The Victor modern Italy is the Victor Emmanuel Monument Emmanuel in Rome (Fig. 104). This is the work of a brilliant Monument, Rome. young sculptor—M. Angelo Lanelli. It is a remarkable conception, but as in so much continental work at the present time, the ornament runs riot, appearing more like the enrichment of a sugared cake than the ornamentation of a masonry structure.

In this case, rectangular forms are used for the main lines of the design, except for a few short lengths of connecting walls and similar features. In spite of its enormous size, it maintains a reasonable scale, and the relation of the various parts is well managed. The figure of King Victor, placed in the centre of the architectural mass and backed by the lines of the colonnade, is given great importance without the necessity of using a gigantic scale; but the large figure beneath, symbolic of Rome, seems a little inclined to compete with it in value and interest. The head and helmet of the latter are a particularly fine piece of modelling, designed upon broad lines with great plain surfaces in every way excellent. Portions of the great relief band around the base are equally good.

Fig. 104. The Victor Emmanuel Monument, Rome.

In the sketch-model, quadrigas are suggested upon the two end pavilions, and these would undoubtedly improve the composition.

The lack of a plain, contrasting surface in this design is badly felt in spite of the sympathetic rhythm of the colonnade. There is no place upon which the eye can find rest—steps, balustrades, groups, lamps, and flag standards cover the whole available space without relief of any kind.

America has recently produced one or two examples of large monumental schemes showing much refinement and a certain amount of imagination, although they have not managed to achieve the magnificent qualities of the best German work.

The design which gained the first prize in the Robert Fulton The Robert Memorial Competition (Fig. 105) has a simplicity Fulton Memorial, and directness of composition which attracts atten- New York. tion. The principal feature is the great flight of steps leading up from the river. These steps, upon a matter of principle, seem to challenge criticism. At any period, so vast a range to climb would have been a trying experience, and in these days of lifts and other means of rapid transit from floor to floor they seem altogether out of place. Apart from this, the relation of the three colonnades—one at the top and two at the water-level defining the harbour—group together very well, and the use of the roof of the lower ones as a promenade is much to be commended.

Pavilions enclosing the landing-stages at the sides furnish these features satisfactorily, and define the boundaries of the scheme, and this idea of enclosure is further developed by the projection of the breakwaters with their terminating posts. The combination of utilitarian purpose with a monumental scheme is to be commended. Not only does it give a practical reason for erection, but it insures the constant presence of people around and about the precincts of the group. A large architectural structure not properly populated is a most depressing object. Romantic interest may be imparted to deserted ruins by a feeling of solitude and isolation, but a complete and perfect building uninhabited is the personification of waste and uselessness, however great its beauty, or however irreproachable the reasons which called it into existence.

The soldiers' and sailors' monument at New York (Fig. 106) is The soldiers' one of those schemes based upon well-known master- and sailors' monument, pieces of ancient architecture of which the Americans New York. have recently given many excellent transcriptions.

Fig. 105. The Robert Fulton Memorial, New York.

Fig. 106. The Soldiers' and Sailors' Monument, New York.

The inspiration of the monument of Lysicrates at Athens is quite obvious, yet the monument is not a mere pedantic copy; the scale alone would perhaps preclude the possibility of this,

Fig. 107.   Detail of the Entrance Door, Soldiers' and Sailors' Monument,
New York.

but there are many departures in other ways. The entrance-door (Fig. 107), plain and simple in conception and treatment, possesses a charm and distinction of its own; the American

symbol of the eagle is well placed in the centre, and crowns the
group in a very pleasing manner.   The rich circle of rusticated

Fig. 108. The Albert Memorial, London.

masonry forming the basement storey to the order is in some ways
an improvement upon the square block of the Greek prototype,

and the arrangement of terraces and steps raising the whole group well up from the surrounding ground gives it prominence and distinction.   The central portion of the design is in white marble, and rises to a height of 100 ft., a proportion of three diameters. The surrounding park-land has been specially laid out for some distance, so that the monument is not merely an isolated incident but becomes a definite part of the general landscape.

London has two great memorial groups, both belonging to the Victorian era—one half-way through and the other right at the end of the reign of the great Queen—commemorating the glorious epoch during which she governed.

The Albert Memorial (Fig. 108)—the earlier example—was

The Albert Memorial, London. designed in a most unfortunate era of English artistic history.   The country had been torn by a succession of revivals of periods with ideals that led upon dissimilar and widely separated paths.   The plain, severe surfaces of the Greek had given place to the broken lines and crowded interest of the Goth ; it is hardly surprising, therefore, to find sculpture and architecture, which seem far removed from each other in aim and character, forming part of the same monument. The Gothic canopy crowned by a spire and pinnacles ornamented with coloured mosaic and decorated with shafts and carved foliage, makes the groups of sculpture which adorn various parts of the terraces and steps seem quite foreign to their surroundings. These groups—representing Europe, Asia, Africa and America— are designed upon purely classic lines, although they are not in any way archaic, and in detail have quite a Greek feeling in the treatment of the drapery and the features of the figures.   The same may be said of the animals which are used to symbolise each continent.   Apart from the incongruous nature of some of the detail and the somewhat unpleasant colouring of the tile paving, the general scheme is in many ways a striking composition   The broad simplicity of the lay-out is one of the finest features of its kind to be found in monumental architecture in this country; the proportion and placing of the various parts of the design are good and not by any means commonplace, and great value is given to the Prince by the canopy, which is well related to the figure.   One of the bad features of the design is the railing considered necessary to prevent vagrants ascending the steps after closing-time.   It may be doubted if this kind of protection is to-day

Fig. 109. Plan of the Victoria Memorial, London.

an absolute necessity, and it should be **entirely** removed from monumental work.

The Queen Victoria Memorial scheme (Fig. 109), with its

Fig. 110. The Victoria Memorial, London.

fine processional road terminated at one end by a great gateway and at the other by the monument, has a definite purpose which must be considered one of its greatest assets. The introduction of a circle into the plan of the road at Trafalgar Square covering the

change in the axis was a masterly stroke which solved a difficult problem in a most graceful manner. The circle at the other end contributes in a very valuable way to the effect of the monument, and also to the basins which receive the water from the fountains. The main approaches entering the latter circle at three points satisfactorily connect it to the surrounding roadways, but regret must be expressed that it was considered necessary to destroy the carriage-drive which led to Piccadilly and replace it by a grass mound of meaningless shape and insignificant scale, cut up by paltry little paths which cross it at all angles. This road, although it may have been bare, was at least equal in importance to the other features of the scheme, and with judicious planting could have been made quite effective without depriving it of its purpose as a carriage-way. Also it could, if necessary, have been reserved for the use of Royal residents in the Palace. The marble group in the centre of this circular Place is now rather in competition with the central feature of the Palace front, which comes immediately upon its axis (Fig. 110). It would have been a great improvement if this central pavilion could have been subdued and the two side wings increased in importance.

The sculpture itself contains much excellent detail, but the crowning group hardly expresses the calm repose and steadfast purpose which characterised the reign of the great Queen, and a quieter design would have been rather more consistent with the qualities which contributed to her greatness.

The few opportunities which have occurred in England for monumental design upon a large scale show that when the necessity arises the artist is not found to be wanting, and the success achieved, coupled with the rapid development which is taking place in English sculpture, seems to promise that future designs of this kind will be at least equal to, if they do not surpass, the work which is in progress in other countries.

CHAPTER IX

CONCLUSION

As was suggested in the first chapter, there seems very little probability at the present day of one artist practising successfully both as a sculptor and an architect. The rising level of modern attainment leads in the opposite direction and each man must specialise more and more in the particular branch of activity in which he is engaged.

In these circumstances, the only possible way of achieving sympathy in the work of two artists is for each to have a knowledge of the requirements and limitations of the other, and to make the necessary allowances.

Perhaps the best time for this intercourse to begin is in the training schools when men are young. Ideals are then high, the sordid interests and practical limitations of commercialism have not as yet sullied the brightness of the imagination of youth. Energy and enthusiasm are potent factors able to carry the fiery spirit to any heights; all obstacles are but spurs to success and the most difficult problems are tackled without thought of the possibility of failure, nay more, with certainty of success.

Intercourse in the schools.

Later in life the practising architect is harassed by clients and builders, bills of quantities and specifications, and the sculptor is endeavouring to satisfy refractory committees, and has his mind occupied with numerous works already in hand in various stages of completion, and neither has time to give thought and earnest study to things which are not of vital necessity to his craft.

Unfortunately in the schools this necessity of mutual understanding is given no recognition. In the chief architectural school of London—that of the Royal Academy—intercourse between sculptors and architects is of the most meagre kind, consisting of

such knowledge as may be gained by a possible chance acquaint-
anceship.

Anything in the nature of systematic visits of architects to the
sculptors' studio—or of sculptors to the architectural studio—is
unheard of. If it were only realised how great a gain would result
in after-life to men of both professions, were each to begin with a
very real and personal knowledge of the work of the other, this
state of affairs would very soon be a thing of the past.

Architecture ought to be a subject of compulsory study for all
sculptors and some acquaintance with modelling should be gained
by all students of architecture.

The knowledge of personality, temperament, aims and purpose
The selection thus gained in the schools would also often be
of a partner. invaluable afterwards when selecting a partner for
collaboration.

The selection of a partner should receive careful consideration.
With the best intentions in the world, it is exceeding difficult for
men having opposite aims and different views to work harmoniously together. And even if they work well in double harness as
far as temperament is concerned, the work of the sculptor will
appear foreign to its position, whatever care is taken to eliminate
the defect, if his usual type of work differs very much from that
of the architect. If possible, a man should be selected who works
upon similar lines, and who goes about his work following a similar
method. The scheme should then proceed in that harmonious
fashion which is so much to be desired.

Then later arises the very difficult point as to who should be
The placing given the design of the monument. Hitherto it has
of the Com- generally been the practice to give it to a sculptor,
mission. and this practice has certain points in its favour. The
great drawback is that (in many cases at least) the sculptor undoubtedly has not so wide an outlook as the architect. The
sculptor's whole attention is given to the design, study and perfection of the figure, and so much does the mind become affected by
constant practice that this has a great tendency to concentrate all
the critical faculties upon the sculpture alone and to prevent a
proper realisation of the whole group. Sculptors will frequently
quote a monument as an excellent piece of work because the
modelling of the figure has surmounted some practical difficulty
in a particularly clever manner. The detail of the architecture

may be exceedingly bad, but it will pass unnoticed and without criticism.

Would it not be better to appoint both a sculptor and an archi-

The appoint-
ment of both a
sculptor and
an architect.
tect for every monument? Let the architect work in co-operation with the sculptor, and upon all points relating to the attitude, the detail and the arrange-ment of the drapery in the figure or group accept his superior knowledge and experience without question. The sculptor should also have an absolutely free hand in the final treatment of the detail. The best result will probably be produced if small-scale drawings embodying the whole scheme are first prepared by the architect, then a sketch-model put up by the sculptor, and the design thereafter developed upon the model. The final full size, with the exception of the contour of the mouldings, should be left entirely in the hands of the sculptor.

Let the keynote of every serious artist be long and consistent

Conclusion.
study. Let him have the highest aims and ideals from the day when his first great work is given to the world to the time when pencil and modelling tool must be laid down never to be handled again. If these things are kept ever in the forefront, if the lamp of enthusiasm does not burn dim nor the zeal nor energy abate, there are no heights impossible to scale, no problems too difficult for solution, and above all, the satisfaction of good work accomplished to the utmost of one's ability will gladden the thoughts of old age, giving them a sweetness and beauty which it is the lot of no other man to experience.

INDEX

For EU product safety concerns, contact us at Calle de José Abascal, 56–1°,
28003 Madrid, Spain or eugpsr@cambridge.org.

www.ingramcontent.com/pod-product-compliance
Ingram Content Group UK Ltd.
Pitfield, Milton Keynes, MK11 3LW, UK
UKHW010049140625
459647UK00012BB/1709